Unmet Needs:

Child Care for Children with Autism in the United States

GUILLERMO MONTES Ph.D.

Copyright © 2011 Children's Institute, Inc.
All rights reserved.

ISBN: 0615470467
ISBN-13: 9780615470467
Library of Congress Control Number: 2011926307

DEDICATION

This monograph is dedicated to children with autism spectrum disorder. I hope that, in some small way, it will assist all of us to develop a more just society that welcomes you and benefits more from your presence and contributions.

>"Don't be afraid to see what you see." – *Ronald Reagan*

TABLE OF CONTENTS

Dedication	iii
Acknowledgments	ix
Peer Review Process	ix
Disclaimer	x
Executive Summary	**1**
Chapter 1: Need For The Study	**13**
Definition And Prevalence Of ASD	13
Child Care Choices In General	16
Child Care Choices Of Families With Children With Special Needs	18
Child Care Choices For Children With ASD	20
Need To Know More	20
Chapter 2: Theoretical Framework	**23**
Chapter 3: Sample And Methods	**27**
Autism Prevalence In The Sample	28
Post-Hoc Power Calculations	28
Survey	28
Chapter 4: Demographic Characteristics	**31**
Household Characteristics	31
Family Size	32
Education, Income, And Insurance	33
Region Of The Country	33
Comparison Of Individual Children	34
Schooling	34
Behavior Index Profile	35
Summary	36
Chapter 5: Preferences for Child Care	**37**
Summary	38
Chapter 6: Child Care Arrangements	**39**
Regular Child Care Arrangements	39
Households With Weekly Child Care Arrangements	40
Types Of Child Care Arrangements	40
Not Participating In The Child Care Markets	43
Reasons Not To Have Child Care	43

Comparison Of Individual Children	45
Lack Of Needed Services	45
Response From Systems To Child's Behavior	46
Victimization By Bullying and Receiving Improper Treatment	47
Summary	48

Chapter 7: Budget Constraint Information — 49

Difficulty Paying For Child Care	50
Summary	51

Chapter 8: Assessing the Supply of Child Care — 53

Chapter 9: Unmet Child Care Needs — 55

Unmet Child Care Needs	55
Last-Minute Child Care Arrangements	56
A Sign Of Difficult Choices: Leaving Children Behind	57
Persistent Concerns About Child Care	58
Summary	59

Chapter 10: Impact Of Unmet Child Care Needs On The Family — 61

Employment Status	61
Child Care-Induced Changes In Employment	63
Child Care-Induced Parental Stress	66
Parenting	67
Sources Of Parental Advice	69
Parental Illness	70
Summary	71

Chapter 11: What Have We Learned — 73

Main Findings Of The Study	73
Directions For Future Research In The Context Of The IACC	76
Directions For Future Research	78
Methodological Lessons	79
Limitations Of The Study	80

Chapter 12: Developing Suggested Policy Strategies — 81

Review Of Child Care Policies	82
Welfare State Models	82
The Current Child Care Policy Framework	85
The Parental Response To Policy: Voice, Exit, And Loyalty	103
A Hirschmannian Analysis	104
Suggested Policy Strategies	110
List Of Abbreviations	115
References	117

TABLE OF FIGURES

Figure 1. Theoretical framework for the study.   23
Figure 2. Selected demographics of the sample.   31
Figure 3. Number of children in the household.   32
Figure 4. Education, income and type of health insurance.   33
Figure 5. Schooling of focal child.   34
Figure 6. Differences in behavior problem index subscales.   35
Figure 7. Importance of ratings of child care attributes.   37
Figure 8. Households with weekly child care arrangements.   39
Figure 9. Child care settings.   41
Figure 10. Content of activities.   42
Figure 11. Reasons not to have a regular child care arrangement.   44
Figure 12. Child received all needed services.   45
Figure 13. Expulsions and suspensions from child care and school.   46
Figure 14. Victimization by peers and improper treatment by staff.   47
Figure 15. Would have made same child care choices if income doubled.   49
Figure 16. Difficulty paying for child care.   50
Figure 17. Supply of child care in the community.   53
Figure 18. Unmet child care needs and needs for respite care.   55
Figure 19. Made last-minute arrangements in the last month.   56
Figure 20. Went to work when should have stayed with child.   57
Figure 21. Persistent concerns about child care.   58
Figure 22. Employment arrangements.   62
Figure 23. Other occupational variables.   63
Figure 24. Child care impacts on employment.   64
Figure 25. Number of employment changes due to child care problems.   65
Figure 26. Relationship between unmet child care needs
  and child care impacts on employment.   66
Figure 27. Child care-related stress at home and at work.   67
Figure 28. Parenting variables.   68
Figure 29. Primary source of parenting advice.   69
Figure 30. Parental illness in the last twelve months.   70

ACKNOWLEDGMENTS

This research was supported in part by the U.S. Administration of Children and Families grant 90YE0102/01 and the Rochester Area Community Foundation.

My sincere appreciation to Pam Montes, Jill Halterman, Dirk Hightower, Bohdan S. Lotyczewski, Marjorie Allan, Janis Cameron, Mary Maiolo, Sean Williams, Shay Hope, Helen Ward, Michael Wischnowski, and Jeannine Eason-Dingus for assistance during the preparation, execution, and peer review of this study.

The opinions and views presented are solely those of the author and are not necessarily those of Children's Institute, Inc., the funders, collaborators, or reviewers.

Other publications related to this grant are:

- Montes, G., Halterman, J. The impact of child care problems on employment: findings from a national survey of US parents. *Academic Pediatrics*, 2011; 11, 80-87.

- Montes, G., Halterman, J. Child care problems and employment among families with preschool-aged children with autism in the United States. *Pediatrics*, 2008; 122, e202-e208.

There are other manuscripts related to this grant currently under peer review.

PEER REVIEW PROCESS

This monograph was reviewed by six colleagues from a variety of fields including the medical, educational, and child care research fields. Additionally, the monograph was reviewed by two parents of children with ASD. I thank all reviewers for their candor and suggestions.

DISCLAIMER

The purpose of the book is to present the results of a national study of child care and suggest national-level policy strategies to alleviate reported problems. The author and publisher are not offering any legal, medical, or other professional services advice. While best efforts have been used in preparing this book, the author and publisher make no representations or warranties of any kind and assume no liabilities of any kind with respect to the accuracy or completeness of the contents. Neither the author nor the publisher shall be held liable or responsible to any person or entity with respect to any loss or incidental or consequential damages caused, or alleged to have been caused, directly or indirectly, by the information or programs contained herein. No warranty may be created or extended by sales representatives or written sales materials. Every family is different, and the advice and strategies contained herein may not be suitable for your situation. Use your own prudent judgment.

EXECUTIVE SUMMARY

This study is the most comprehensive exploration of the child care situation for households with a child with ASD in the United States. Although our focus was ages zero to thirteen, most of the children with ASD were school age. There are four major themes:

(1) **Families of children with ASD are much like other families.** Families of children with autism spectrum disorders (ASD) are very much like other families in a number of factors thought to influence the child care decision-making process. In particular, families of children with ASD receive child care services in every community setting and offering. All sectors that offer activities for children, including the religious sector, family care, center care, and tutoring services can expect to come in contact with families of children with ASD.

Like other families, families of children with ASD have strong preferences for well-respected programs that offer engaging learning activities in accessible places at prices they can afford. Like many other families, they have adjusted or modified their employment to meet their child care needs. Those families that decided not to use child care on a regular basis and have a child with ASD give many of the same reasons for their decision that other families in similar situations give. Finally, families of children with ASD were similar in terms of annual income, education, race, and other demographic characteristics (see Table 1).

(2) **Families of children with ASD report much higher levels of unmet need.** There were some very notable differences between the child care experiences of families of children with ASD and other families. Compared with other families, families of children with ASD were three times more likely to report unmet child care needs and needing respite care, eight times more likely to report their children were not receiving all needed services, eight times more likely to report their children were expelled from child care, and five times more likely to report their children were suspended or expelled from schools. When they used child care, they were seven times more likely to have persistent concerns that their children's needs were not being met, and four times more likely to be persistently concerned about negative peer influences.

In some cases, the decision not to use child care was heavily constrained by unavailable supply. Families of children with ASD were ten times more likely to report not using child care because it would not meet their children's needs, and forty-seven times more likely to cite their children's special needs as a reason not to have a weekly child care arrangement. They were eight times less likely to have employment that provided child care.

(3) **Families with ASD are more likely to report that child care problems impact employment.** Compared with other families, families with children with ASD were three times more likely to report that child care problems had resulted in decreased job performance, looking for new jobs, and turning down job offers. They were four times more likely to report quitting a job because of child care problems. They

were five times more likely to report having made employment decisions that negatively impact future employability, and six times more likely to report having stopped looking for work because of child care problems. They were twice as likely to report three or more child care-related employment impacts, and four times as likely to report both unmet child care needs and child care-related employment impacts, compared to other families. They were twice as likely as other families to report that an adult in the household had two jobs.

(4) **Families with children with ASD were more likely to report child care-related high stress** both at home and at work; they were three times more likely to report they had no one to turn to for emotional support, and twice as likely to report not coping well with their parenting role. They were twice as likely to report not using family as a source of parenting advice and five times more likely to report using mental health professionals as a source of parenting advice.

Unmet Needs: Child Care for Children with Autism in the United States.

Area	Families with children with ASD more likely to	Families with children with ASD just as likely to	Families with children with ASD less likely to
Demographics	• Have an older parent • Have more siblings • Child with ASD higher externalizing and internalizing problems • Household has a permanently disabled member • Household has a retired person • Attend specialized schools • Homeschool	• Report comparable: • Annual HH income • Parental education • Gender of respondent • Race of respondent • Two-parent household • Stay-at-home parent • Adult employed in HH • Public insurance • HH has person looking for work	• Attend (regular) public schools • Report employment offers child care • Attend private school
Preferences for child care attributes		• Rate all preference variables as important: cost, location, training, learning activities, etc.	
Child care arrangement	• Have "other" child care arrangement • Participate in tutoring and in programs with behavior control components	• Have a weekly child care arrangement • Attend all forms of child care settings (except "other") • Participate in programs that offer music, art, dance, sports, book club, scouts, etc.	
Reasons not to have a child care arrangement	• Report that the child needs special care • Report that the child care is unable to meet child's needs	• All other reasons for not using child care regularly (prefer to raise child at home, etc.)	
Concerns about child care	• Report repeated concerns about child's needs not met • Report repeated concerns about peer influences on child	• Report repeated concerns about the safety, untrained staff, reliability, and cost of arrangement	
Unmet needs	• Report they needed child care and were unable to get it • Report they needed respite care • Report expulsion of child from child care • Report expulsion or suspension of child from school • Report child bullied • Report improper treatment of child by child care staff	• Report that they felt they should have stayed with their children and went to work anyway	• Report child received all needed services

Executive Summary

Area	Families with children with ASD more likely to	Families with children with ASD just as likely to	Families with children with ASD less likely to
Constraints	• Report difficulty paying for child care	• Report same child care choices if income doubled • Report same choice not to use child care if income doubled	
Supply of child care	• Report the supply of affordable care was good or excellent	• Report other types of community supply of child care was good or excellent	
Child care impact on employment	• Report as a result of child care problems: • Decreased job performance • Turned down job • Stopped looking for work • Made decisions that impact future employability negatively • Quit a job • Multiple child care impacts on employment • To have both unmet child care needs and employment impacts	• Report as a result of child care problems: • Modified job • Absenteeism • Changed schedule	
Child care impact on parental stress	• Report medium or high levels of stress at work because of child care problems • Report medium or high levels of stress at home because of child care problems		
Parenting	• Rely on mental health professionals and others for parenting advice	• Report good or excellent family-work balance • Report parental anxiety, clinical depression, or stress-induced condition	• Report having parenting support • Report coping well with parenting role • Report relying on family or friends for parenting advice

Table 1. Summary of study findings.

Table 1 summarizes the main findings of the study. There are several key conclusions:

(1) **Every community setting that offers activities for children, including religious institutions, dance academies, family child care, tutoring services, and center child care programs, should expect and be prepared to care for children with ASD and their siblings.** Currently, preparations have focused on preparing school settings, particularly at younger ages, to receive children with ASD. It appears that no systematic training or preparation in other settings is occurring. Further, no preparation at all is occurring to accommodate siblings of children with ASD, who present with their own set of issues (Bagenholm and Gillberg 1991; Gold 1993; Mates 1990; Macks and Reeve 2007).

(2) **Families are constrained by a scarce supply of trained caregivers.** Families with ASD reported not participating in care because they could not find affordable care that would meet their children's needs. Families of children with ASD who used care reported being concerned with their child's needs being met. In addition, in this study of child care for mostly school-age children, families of children with ASD were more likely to report expulsions, bullying, and improper treatment by staff. Clearly, there is scarcity of safe care that meets the needs of children with ASD.

(3) **Families of children with ASD report difficulty paying for child care.** In the context of other research studies showing the impact that having a child with ASD has on family finances, there is little doubt that the typical family of a child with ASD needs financial assistance.

(4) **Families of children with ASD need child care assistance to establish and maintain stable employment.** They are

not only more likely to have unmet child care needs, but those unmet needs are more likely to cause multiple, severe impacts on their employment.

(5) **No limitations on parental choice are warranted** because parents of children with ASD want for their children what other parents want for their children. They want full participation in the community, and they look for care within the same child care and activity choices that are available to the rest of the American population.

Given these conclusions, below I list some suggested strategies that will likely improve access to quality child care for families of children with ASD.

First, it is important to implement the American with Disabilities Act (ADA) in child care settings and to provide enough assistance to providers to meet ADA requirements.

    a. **Offer assistance to providers in meeting ADA requirements**. Many providers want to comply with ADA and offer an appropriate environment for children with special needs. They often lack resources, training, and even information about what their obligations are under ADA. Therefore, it makes sense to call for policies that strengthen providers' resources in complying with existing law.

    b. **Consider policies that strengthen the civic and nonprofit sectors**, including the religious nonprofit sector, to assist families to meet their child care needs, particularly for the low-income population and children with special needs. Children with ASD attend all these sectors, and all will need assistance to meet ADA requirements.

c. **Within the context of the Child Care Development Fund (CCDF), consider increased reimbursement for child care providers that are committed to inclusion and are currently serving a child with ASD whose family also meets income eligibility.** Low-income families of children with ASD are very unlikely to establish stable employment unless they can secure stable child care that meets their child's needs. Using some portion of the CCDF funds to incentivize the growth of trained child care providers for children with ASD may effectively assist families of children with ASD to secure better employment.

d. **Make high-quality, cost-effective training available to providers when and where they need it.** There is a need to develop high-quality, cost-effective training that meets the needs of providers. Many child care providers are women- and minority-owned businesses with small profit margins; thus, there is a need to provide the training at a price they can afford. The training needs to be brief and be available when and where it is needed. Because the 1% of children with ASD are geographically distributed throughout the country, the training must use new technologies (e.g., online) so that geographically isolated child care providers can access it when they need it. It would be advantageous if professional organizations were to take a lead role in developing peer support and mentoring approaches in communities to help fellow providers become trained and appropriately use the available trainings across the U.S.

e. **Consider a national hotline to provide individualized mentoring and resources for providers**

needing assistance with ADA compliance, particularly in the areas of managing child behavior and developing executive functioning. With current technology capabilities, such a hotline may be a web-based resource that offers not only information and materials but also direct distance mentoring on how to handle specific situations.

Second, to fully implement ADA, parents must have affordable avenues to pursue the enforcement of their children's rights.

    a. **Form legal defense organizations** that are able to provide legal representation to parents of children with ASD at relatively low cost. No one is promoting litigation for its own sake. Unfortunately, sometimes litigation or the credible threat of litigation is needed to get compliance with ADA.

    b. **Encourage parents of children with ASD to report violations of ADA to the U.S. Department of Justice.** Autism organizations can provide essential information to parents of their rights under ADA and how to report violations. It is essential that the U.S. government become aware of how large a problem exists, both to evaluate needs for training at the national level and because the current unmet needs are invisible to most of the political community.

    c. **Facilitate changes in social norms regarding ADA and autism among child care providers.** Initially, this can be done by clarifying the obligations of child care providers under ADA with respect to children with special needs or behavioral problems, including ASD, or both, through the CCDF and the U.S. Department of Justice. Eventually, parents' groups and the general media can convey the message that expulsion is not an acceptable solution for children with ASD.

Third, families of children with ASD need financial assistance.

    a. Legislatively, **consider a federal special needs child tax credit** to assist families of children with ASD or other disabilities who have more expenditures and higher loss of income than comparable families in part because of the impact that child care has on their employment.

Fourth, resolve the conflict of interest implicit in the Individuals with Disabilities Education Act (IDEA), which is presently starving communities from receiving funds and providing needed services.

    a. Currently, public schools are beneficiaries of their own adjudication decisions regarding services for children with ASD under IDEA. The current policy starves community settings of both funds and providers, makes schools the focus of litigation to expand services to the community, and generally conceptualizes ASD as disability that should receive treatment only if it affects classroom behavior or academic achievement. Also, it does not always serve the child in the least restrictive environment, which may be the community setting during non-school hours. Obviously, **a better balance must be reached between school and community because the child with ASD continues to have needs beyond the school hours.**

Regarding future research, I recommend including a member of the Child Care Bureau in future Interagency Autism Coordinating

Committee (IACC) strategic planning rosters to ensure coordination between child care and autism research, as well as to provide context for future federal policies both in ASD and child care. In addition, the IACC may consider calling for research that develops effective, community-based interventions for children with ASD in child care or community settings, particularly in light of the geographically disaggregated nature of ASD prevalence and the global trend for inclusion of children with special needs in all community settings.

CHAPTER 1: NEED FOR THE STUDY

DEFINITION AND PREVALENCE OF ASD

Autism spectrum disorders (ASDs) are a form of pervasive developmental disorders (PDD) characterized by impaired social communication and repetitive behaviors. ASDs include autistic disorder (Kanner 1943), Asperger's syndrome (AS), and pervasive developmental disorder—not otherwise specified (PDD-NOS). ASDs vary in severity dramatically, so that each child presents a somewhat unique profile of the disorder. Because of this feature of ASDs, generalizations on what the child can or cannot accomplish based on the diagnosis alone are unwise. There are no genetic or blood tests for ASD, and currently the disorder is defined exclusively based on behavior using a combination of professional and parental observation. Many children with ASD have comorbid disorders such as attention deficit hyperactivity disorder, anxiety disorders, epilepsy, or mental retardation.

The prevalence of ASD in the United States nears 1%, with males being four times more likely to have ASD than females, for unknown reasons (Centers for Disease Control and Prevention (CDC) 2009). ASD has a heritability estimate of 80% (Kendler 2010), and ASD siblings are at higher risk of having the disorder (Constantino et al. 2010). Thus, it is not unusual, among larger families, to have several children with ASD.

The prevalence of ASD has been rising for unknown reasons since the 1960s (Fommbonne 2003). In the United States, there was a 57% increase in prevalence of ASDs from 2002 to 2006 (Centers for Disease Control and Prevention (CDC) 2009). Although there is little doubt that changes in diagnostic criteria and methods of ascertainment, including increased parental awareness, explain some of the increase (King and Bearman 2009; Blaxill 2004), perhaps up to 40%, there is emerging consensus that at least some of the increase represents a true increase in the number of cases rather than improved detection methods. The rise of autism cases is a global phenomenon, although studies have found evidence of spatial clustering with increased prevalence in relatively small geographic areas (Mazumdar et al. 2009). Today, the causes of ASDs are unknown, although a variety of genetic, epigenetic (Interagency Autism Coordinating Committee 2009), and environmental hypotheses are being considered.

The increase in ASD cases has profound public policy implications as every nation struggles to determine how to best serve these children within its particular welfare state model. In the United States, because of its decentralized educational framework and its reliance on private health markets, much of the conversation has focused on how states can provide better services for children with ASD (Saunders 2010) and simultaneously on what changes need to occur in insurance coverage for families with children with ASD (Holland 2010; Bouder, Spielman, and Mandell 2009).

Meanwhile, parents of children with ASD have litigated to force schools to comply with the provisions of the Individuals with Disabilities Education Act (IDEA), particularly in light of the 2000 National Council on Disabilities report on IDEA implementation in schools (National Council on Disabilities 2000) and the 2009 Government Accountability Office (GAO) report on abuse in public and private schools. This report highlighted the plight of children with disabilities in American schools and treatment centers.

In particular, the GAO report publicized the case of a four-year-old child with ASD and cerebral palsy who was "restrained in a wooden chair with leather straps—described as resembling a miniature electric chair—for being 'uncooperative'." Although the school board was found liable, the teachers were not. Indeed, the GAO reported one still worked at the school in 2009 (United States Government Accountability Office 2009). In this context, the fact that the IDEA report cards published by the U.S. Department of Education consistently show that the majority of the United States and its territories fail to achieve their self-imposed IDEA compliance goals (U.S. Department of Education 2008) is not reassuring. Unfortunately, the need for litigation is ongoing.

Yet, the vast majority of children with ASD spend less than half of their childhoods in public educational settings, spending more time at home and in a variety of child care arrangements. There is very little scientific knowledge about how families with children with ASD make decisions for child care and where these children spend their time. Thus, the focus of this study is to reduce this gap in the literature and to suggest reasonable policy strategies, well adapted to the current ways in which the United States provides child care assistance, that would make child care more welcoming to children with ASD. The goal is to get as close to full participation as feasible.

This study investigates family child care decisions for all children within the family. Many children with ASD have siblings. The research on the adjustment of siblings of children with ASD is in its infancy, with some studies showing adverse effects for non-disabled siblings of children with ASD and others showing normal functioning (Bagenholm and Gillberg 1991; Gold 1993; Mates 1990). Further research has discovered that demographic risk factors, such as lower income or being a two-child family versus having more children, may moderate the impact of being a sibling of a child with ASD on outcomes (Macks and Reeve 2007). Thus, siblings of children with ASD in certain demographic groups may present salient psychological and academic profiles that merit intervention.

In the next section, we first provide a brief review of how parents make child care choices, then specifically focus on how parents of children with special needs make child care choices, and finally we review the only study that investigates this topic for families of children with ASD.

CHILD CARE CHOICES IN GENERAL

Many theories and approaches have been advanced to explain how parents choose child care. The most widely accepted theory relies on a general rational choice framework positing that parents maximize their preferences given budgetary and time constraints. The framework was developed by economists, coming out of the efforts to model the labor participation decisions of working mothers. Consequently, much empirical research has concentrated on testing the predictions of this model, particularly for working mothers of young children. For example, research in the last decade confirmed that higher child care prices are negatively related to the labor supply of married mothers and to the likelihood of using paid care; conversely, subsidies can be used to affect these parental choices (Blau 2001; Blau and Robins 1998; Blau and Tekin 2007; Michalopoulos and Robins 2002). Much research explores how mothers respond to child care price changes and subsidies, as well as the larger societal determinants of child care choice (Blau 2001; Blau and Robins 1998; Cleveland, Gunderson, and Hyatt 1996; Connelly and Kimmel 2003; Fuller, Holloway, and Liang 1996; Han and Waldfogel 2001; NICHD Early Child Care Research Network 1997; Powell 2002). A number of studies concentrated on the role of child care during the welfare-to-work transition, particularly for mothers of young children (Kimmel 1995; Blau and Tekin 2007; Danziger, Ananat, and Browning 2006; United States Administration for Children and

Families 2007). Not surprisingly, studies found great differences by socioeconomic status, with upper-income families being able to secure high-quality care, and low-income families, sharing similar preferences for quality, unable to access the same level of care due to affordability, availability, and schedule flexibility barriers (Brandon and Hofferth 2003; Larner and Phillips 1994). In this regard, the proportion of income spent in child care varies greatly by the families' socioeconomic position, with poor families spending an average of 35%, compared with 7% for non-poor families (Smith 2000).

Following the rational choice framework, researchers have typically conceptualized child care as a decision (a) on the arrangement of an individual child, (b) largely determined by the age of the child, (c) highly constrained by income status, and (d) whose focus of interest is either maternal employment or child developmental status, or both. Preferences for child care settings or attributes are considered exogenous and stable. Consequently, many studies were conducted as if the child were the only child of the family and the mother were the sole decision-maker with a focus on budgetary or time constraint variables rather than determinants of preferences. Similarly, many studies concentrated on the specific age of the child divided into well-established subgroups (e.g. preschool, infant care). Finally, because parents do not choose quality as defined by experts, there have been many attempts to understand why this is so and what mechanisms (e.g. quality rating systems, subsidies) will aid parents in viewing quality as professionals do (Emlen 2010; Ryan et al. 2011; Rose and Elicker 2008; Larner and Phillips 1994).

In addition to the rational choice model and its variations, there are other, less popular, approaches to child care decision making. Emlen (Emlen 2010) hypothesized that flexibility in both employment and child care arrangements is the essential factor to balance work, family life, and child care (Hill, Hawkins, et al. 2004;

Tausig and Fenwick 2001; Hill, Martinson, et al. 2004; Clark 2001; Greenhaus, Collins, and Shaw 2003). Meyers and Jordan view child care choices as contextualized decisions that often reproduce economic and social stratification patterns present in society (Meyers and Jordan 2006). Finally, quite recently, there has been an attempt to integrate these various perspectives with the work of behavioral economists and cognitive psychologists. The integrative accommodation approach integrates the essence of the rational choice framework but modifies it in two important aspects: (a) preferences are endogenous and subject to change and are thought to be particularly vulnerable to social norming and social network effects, and (b) instead of maximization, consumers of child care are thought to use a number of cognitive shortcuts or heuristic approaches in making their child care decisions. The integrative accommodation model has not yet been subjected to empirical testing but deserves serious consideration in the design of future empirical studies (Chaudry, Henly, and Meyers 2010).

CHILD CARE CHOICES OF FAMILIES WITH CHILDREN WITH SPECIAL NEEDS

There is a paucity of research on the child care choices of families with children with disabilities. Since the deinstitutionalization of children with disabilities (Zigler and Lang 1991; Buysse et al. 1999), children with disabilities have been cared by families. As early as 1991, however, it was known that parents of children with disabilities face additional barriers when selecting child care, ranging from prejudice and fear about providing services for a child with a disability to inadequate numbers of trained caregivers (Zigler and Lang 1991).

Families of children with special needs face child care and employment challenges at higher rates than the general population (Ward et al. 2006; Rosenzweig et al. 2008; Rosenzweig, Brennan, and

Ogilivie 2002). In 2000, the earliest nationally representative study of working mothers with children with disabilities found that the presence of behavioral or emotional problems predicted hours of child care use (Brandon 2000). A subsequent nationally representative study concluded that mothers of children with special needs had lower rates of employment and higher employment instability than mothers in the general population (Ward et al. 2006). This finding corroborated previous small-scale studies (Cuskelly, Pulman, and Hayes 1998; Shearn and Todd 2000). The context for some of these findings is a related literature that has demonstrated that if the child exhibits behavior problems, he or she is likely to be expelled from care in a variety of settings, including public preschool (Gilliam and Shahar 2006; Buck and Ambrosino 2004). Another nationally representative study, published in 2005, found that parents of children with disabilities used very low-cost care, which raises questions about the need for targeted subsidies and the quality of the care (Parish et al. 2005). Many of these studies concentrated exclusively on children too young to attend kindergarten.

Little is known about child care options for school-age children with disabilities. A nationally representative study found that other variables may moderate the relationship between the presence of disability and child care use. In particular, disability was found to be associated with lower child care use for single-parent households but not for two-parent households, who had markedly lower usage (Parish and Cloud 2005). In addition, mothers of children with special needs older than six years old were more likely to have unstable job arrangements or no job at all than all other groups of mothers, as reported in a tri-state study (Ward et al. 2006). Some studies have linked parental concerns about after-school care with parental stress and poor psychological well-being (Barnett and Gareis 2006).

Much of what is known about the child care choices parents of children with special needs make comes from a multi-source, multi-method study in the state of Maine conducted by Helen Ward and her colleagues (2006). This study found that parents of children with special needs were more likely to have unstable child care, have child care that did not meet the needs of the child or where the child was not included in activities, have lower levels of labor force participation, and report myriad work problems related to caring for their child with special needs. In families with several children with special needs or children with special needs that had a behavioral component, the outcomes for parental employment and stability of child care were even worse. Importantly, in Ward's survey of child care providers, she found that providers expressed willingness to care for children with special needs but reported lacking resources, training, and funding to accommodate their needs.

CHILD CARE CHOICES FOR CHILDREN WITH ASD

Very little is known about how families of children with ASD in the United States make child care decisions. A survey of the literature revealed only one nationally representative study on preschool-age children, which uses the National Survey of Children's Health, 2003 (Montes and Halterman 2008). This study showed that families of children with ASD were seven times more likely to report child care caused employment problems even though attendance to preschool was high. This provides strong evidence that the child care needs of families with preschool-age children with ASD are not adequately met in the United States.

NEED TO KNOW MORE

Given the needs of families with children with ASD, it is quite surprising how little interest and research there is on the topic of child care arrangements for children with autism spectrum disorders. There is a need for further study to establish some basic information regarding child care settings, unmet child care needs, and impact of unmet child care needs on parental stress and employment. The previous nationally representative study was limited in that it focused only on preschool-age children. There are many good reasons to believe that families with children with ASD experience problems in securing child care at other ages.

CHAPTER 2:
THEORETICAL FRAMEWORK

Figure 1 displays the theoretical framework of the study. The theoretical framework here is influenced by the rational choice literature that views child care decisions as solutions to maximization of exogenous preferences subject to constraints (Blau 2001; Chaudry, Henly, and Meyers 2010).

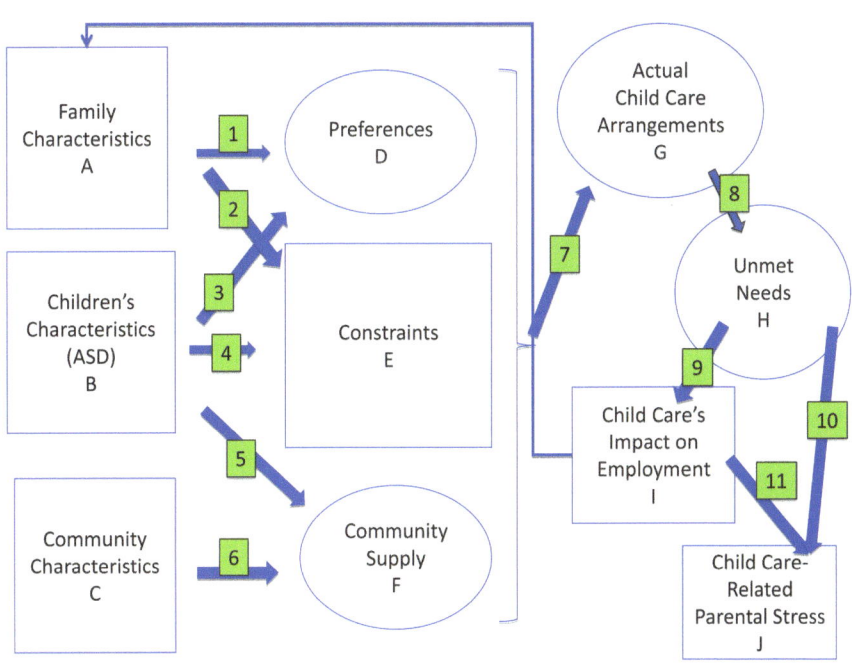

FIGURE 1. THEORETICAL FRAMEWORK FOR THE STUDY.

Family and child characteristics (A & B) thought to influence the child care decision include whether the family is a single-parent family, maternal employment, the number of children, annual income, parental education, age of the child, and the like. In the context of this monograph, the presence of a child with ASD is the critical independent variable.

Community characteristics (C) matter not only because of the availability and quality of the community supply of child care (represented by arrow 6) but also because different communities may have different social norms about the care of children.

Consistent with the standard rational choice model, preferences (D) about child care attributes are assumed to be exogenous and stable (Chaudry, Henly, and Meyers 2010).

Time and budget constraints (E) are ubiquitous. A child care solution that is not affordable or does not meet time constraints, including transportation, is not a viable solution. Thus, families with fewer resources both financially and in terms of disposable time have more constrained decision-making. Time constraints and financial constraints are interdependent. For one thing, low-income workers typically lack job flexibility. Other influences are the number of children, the costs of transportation, and many other household variables, including general household organizational skills. Single-parent families are more constrained on both time and budget fronts, as are families without access to relatives willing to care for children, families with more complex needs (e.g. health problems for parents or children), and families with more demanding or inflexible jobs.

Another set of constraints that strongly shapes parental behavior is informational constraints. Parents are assumed to want information but not at any cost. Cost in information processing stems from various sources: complexity of the information, contamination of the information with error, ease or difficulty in processing and evaluating the information (e.g. literacy, critical analysis, familiarity with informational systems, etc.), and financial and time resources to access the information. Given the informational constraints in American society, one would expect that parents with scarce time, with barriers to literacy, who need assistance from complex systems, or who live in communities where reliable information is mixed with myths would not invest as many of their own resources in becoming informed about child care options, compared to parents who can process information faster, have time and money to facilitate access, do not need assistance from complex systems, or live in communities where reliable information is more widely disseminated. These informational structures invariably result in highly educated parents not only accessing and having more relevant information but also investing more resources in obtaining additional information than lower-income parents, *even if their preferences for information are identical.* It is a textbook case of increasing returns to scale: the higher informational capacity, the larger investment in information acquisition.

Many of these constraints stem from the general informational structure of modern society, and thus we see the same informational pattern in almost all important life decision-making processes, such as health care decisions, college decision-making, getting a mortgage, and the like. One of the returns of higher education is to lower informational barriers for all major life decisions. Thus, a college education makes it less costly to obtain additional information later on, and the societal disparities between informational haves and have-nots widen. The result is that accurate information considered obvious in one community may be seriously questioned as a myth in another. In an environment where the costs of separating useful information from myth are high, it makes sense to invest resources in non-informational activities that have comparatively higher returns. Thus, the cycle reinforces itself, and informational disparities widen more.

The community supply is determined by community characteristics alone but also varies depending on whether the family has a child who requires different care from the normally developing norm (arrow 5).

Given preferences and constraints, parents decide on actual arrangements for their children. It is possible for families to make the best possible choices, as they define best, and yet report unmet child care needs. These unmet needs then may impact employment decisions and also result in higher stress. Any child care-related employment decisions then feed back by changing the family characteristics (e.g. from full-time work to part-time work).

This theoretical framework is used to organize the presentation of results in the following chapters.

CHAPTER 3: SAMPLE AND METHODS

The current study was part of a longitudinal study of families' child care decision-making in the United States (Montes and Halterman 2011). Participants were recruited from the Gallup Panel, a U.S. nationally representative random-digit dial survey research panel. Our sample is a subset of eligible households, having a child in the ages birth to thirteen years old, that consented to participate in the study. The study also recruited an oversample of households with a child with autism spectrum disorders by inviting to the study members of the Gallup Panel with a known case of ASD in the household. The survey was completed on the phone in English, and both the general sample and ASD subsample completed the same survey under the same conditions during the fall of 2009. The response rate was 70.1%. The study was approved by the University of Rochester's Research Subjects Review Board.

The analytical sample for this study uses the first survey of data collection. The Gallup Organization provided post-stratification weights based on census region, income level, and highest level of education obtained by any adult in the household, based on estimates from the Census Population Survey. Weights for the ASD subpopulation were calculated based on income, education, and region estimates for the ASD subpopulation from the National Survey of Children's Health, 2003. After post-stratification weights were calculated, the ASD oversample was weighted appropriately to represent its prevalence on the U.S. population. All analyses were conducted using SPSS and Stata. Household analyses are weighted, and focal child analyses are unweighted. Cross tabulations using designed corrected F statistics were used for most analyses. Bivariate odd ratios were calculated from the percentages reported in the charts. Unless otherwise specified, the charts measure the percentage of households or focal children.

AUTISM PREVALENCE IN THE SAMPLE

The prevalence of ASD in this study was 0.8% (95% confidence interval 0.5%-1.1%), well within the prevalence rates of recently published studies (Centers for Disease Control and Prevention (CDC) 2009).

POST-HOC POWER CALCULATIONS

Because the sample for children with ASD was only fifty-six persons, there was concern that there would be insufficient statistical power to detect differences between the ASD and non-ASD groups. Indeed, post-hoc power calculations revealed sufficient power to detect differences in proportions between the groups of 20% (with the control group at 50%), at the standard 0.05 significance level. As the results in the subsequent chapters evidence, there were many findings at high levels of significance because the differences between the groups in many variables are so strikingly large. Nevertheless, it is quite probable that the study lacked sufficient power to detect smaller differences between the ASD and general population groups that may have policy significance.

SURVEY

The survey had several parts: basic demographics, child care arrangements, preferences and assessment of community supply, reasons not to have a regular (defined as weekly) child care arrangement, health conditions of the child, child care impact on the family and employment, and a specific child assessment on a focal child. The focal child assessment was an attempt to select the child whose child care was most likely to cause employment problems. The focal child was either the only child in the household, the child whose child care arrangement was having the most impact on employment changes (identified by parents), or, if parents reported no problems, a randomly chosen child. In households with a child with ASD, the focal child was the child with ASD. If multiple children with ASD lived in the household, the child was picked at random from those who were reported to have ASD. Because the survey was designed and weighted to be a household-level survey, most of the results presented are household-level results. However, in selected sections, we compare the child with ASD with the other focal children.

CHAPTER 4:
DEMOGRAPHIC CHARACTERISTICS

In this chapter, we explore the constructs A (household characteristics) and B (child characteristics) of the theoretical model of Chapter 2.

HOUSEHOLD CHARACTERISTICS

There were 1450 families in the general population and 56 families with a child with ASD. This chapter presents their demographic information.

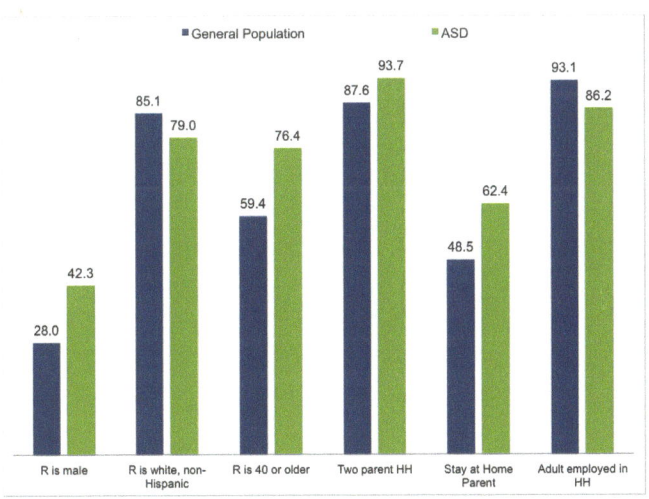

FIGURE 2. SELECTED DEMOGRAPHICS OF THE SAMPLE.
NOTE: R – RESPONDENT, HH – HOUSEHOLD.

The only statistically significant demographic difference was that the respondents of families with children with ASD were more likely to be older (76.4 vs. 59.4, p<.05, OR 2.21). Households were statistically comparable in the other demographic characteristics, although in our sample the ASD group respondents were more likely to be male. Note that the majority of households self-identified as two-parent households with at least one adult employed. Although the rate of self-described "stay at home parents" was high, upon examination, many of those parents were in households reported to have both parents working. Thus, the label 'stay at home' should not be interpreted to mean not working.

FAMILY SIZE

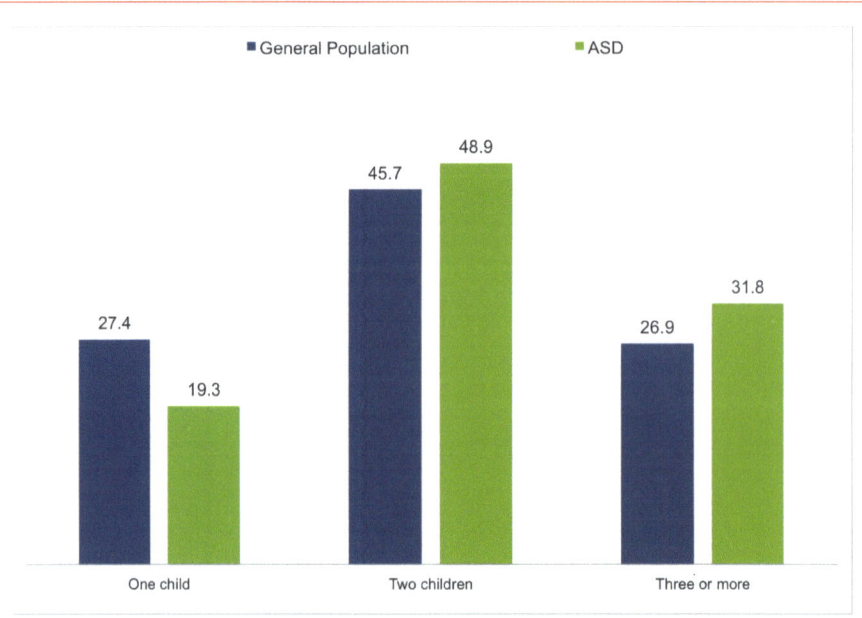

FIGURE 3. NUMBER OF CHILDREN IN THE HOUSEHOLD.

With regards to number of children in the household, families with a child with ASD were less likely to report having a single child and more likely to report having a greater number of children than other families (p<.05).

EDUCATION, INCOME, AND INSURANCE

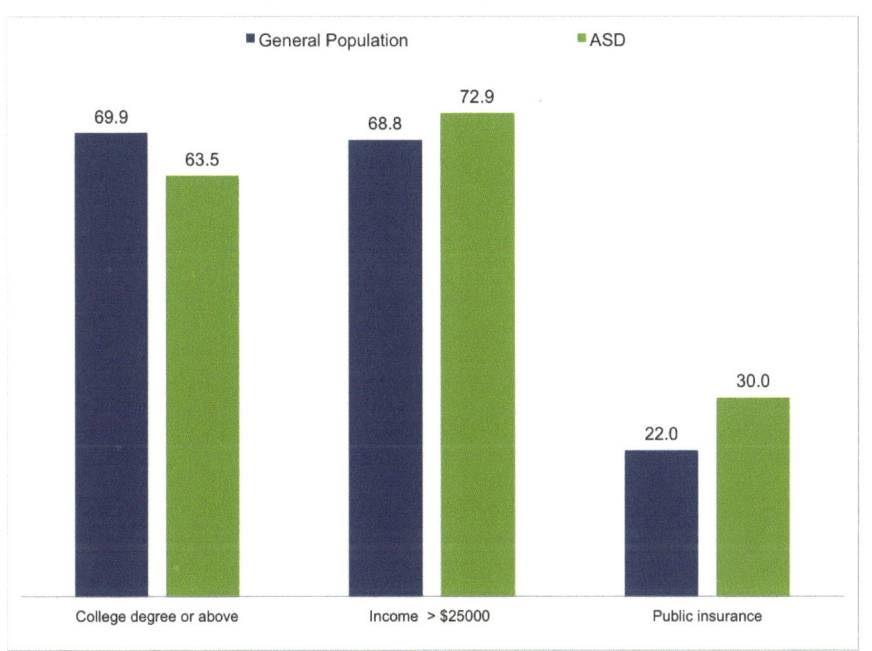

FIGURE 4. EDUCATION, INCOME AND TYPE OF HEALTH INSURANCE.

There were no statistically significant differences between families with children with ASD and the general population in education, household income, or probability of receiving public health insurance.

REGION OF THE COUNTRY

The study covered all regions of the country. There were no significant differences in representation by region of country (Northeast, South, West, Mid-Atlantic) (p>.05).

COMPARISON OF INDIVIDUAL CHILDREN

This subsection presents unweighted comparisons between the child with ASD and other focal children.

SCHOOLING

Parents were asked, "What type of school does this child attend? (a) not in school (e.g. too young), (b) home school, (c) public school, (d) private school, (e) specialized public school for children with special needs, (f) specialized private school for children with special needs."

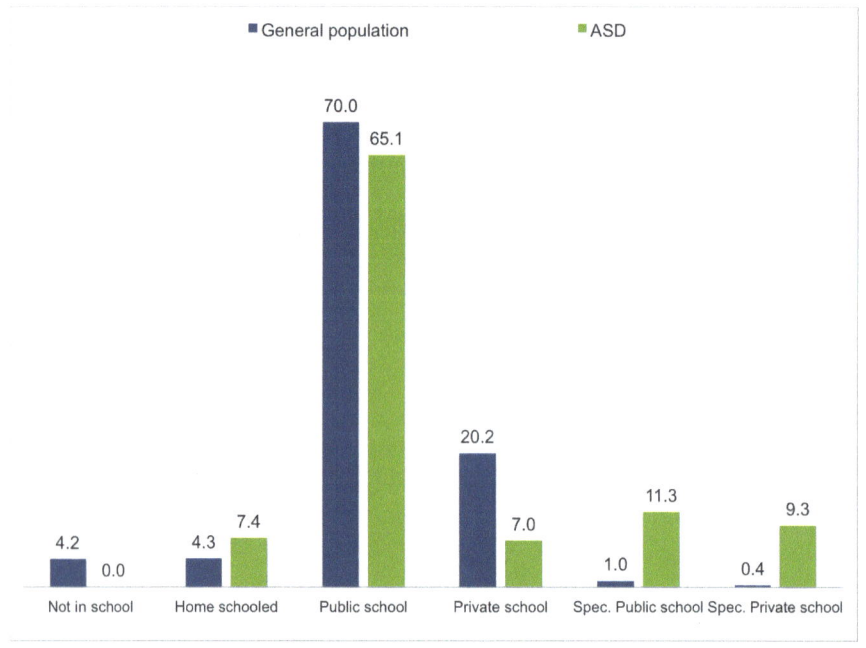

Figure 5. Schooling of focal child.
Note: Spec – specialized.

Although two-thirds of children with ASD attended regular public school, as a group they were more likely to attend public or private specialized schools or be homeschooled (p<.01), and less likely to be enrolled in private schools (OR 0.30, p<.01). Overall, one-third of children with ASD were in one of these alternative settings.

BEHAVIOR INDEX PROFILE

The behavior problem index (BPI) measures internalizing problems and externalizing problems. The alpha reliabilities in our sample were 0.88 for the general sample and 0.84 for the ASD sample for externalizing problems, and 0.73 for the general sample and 0.61 for the ASD sample for internalizing problems. The subscales are constructed so that a higher number would indicate more internalizing or externalizing problems.

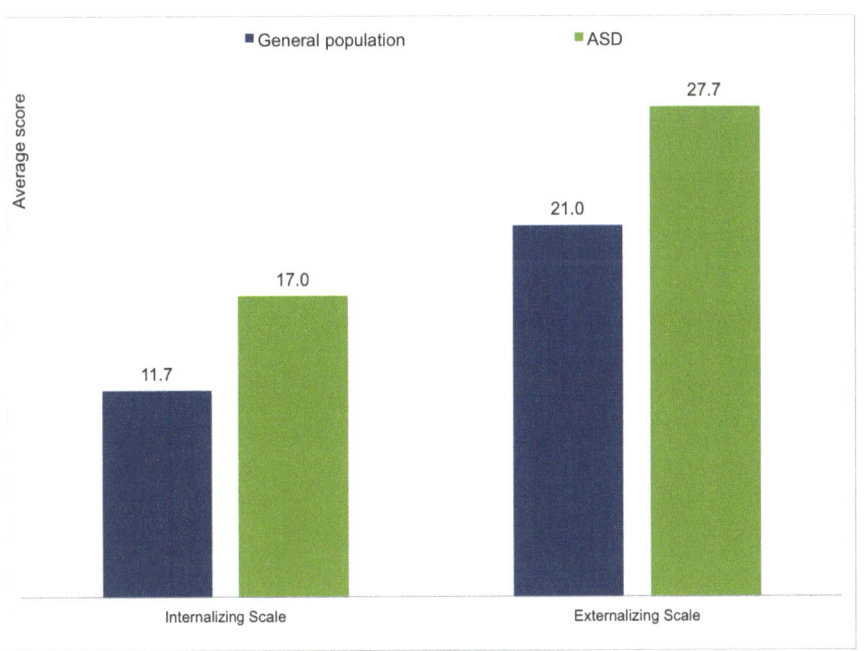

FIGURE 6. DIFFERENCES IN BEHAVIOR PROBLEM INDEX SUBSCALES.

Not surprisingly, children with ASD rated significantly higher in both externalizing and internalizing problems (p<.01).

SUMMARY

In this study, families with children with ASD had educational backgrounds, annual incomes, and family structures similar to those of families in the general population. Families with children with ASD were more likely to have older parents and more siblings. Individually, children with ASD were more likely to present with higher externalizing and internalizing behavior problems than other focal children. Although the majority of children in both groups attended public schools, children with ASD were more likely to be receiving education in other settings than were other focal children.

CHAPTER 5:
PREFERENCES FOR CHILD CARE

This chapter examines the preference construct (D) in the theoretical model.

Parents were asked, "Parents consider a number of different factors when selecting child care arrangements. Please tell me how important each of the following factors is to you, using a scale of very important, somewhat important, not too important, or not important at all. How about (a) the location, (b) the cost, (c) the reliability, (d) the learning activities, (e) the schedule of hours of operation, (f) how a particular activity fits with the family schedule, (g) the reputation of the program, and (h) the training of the staff?"

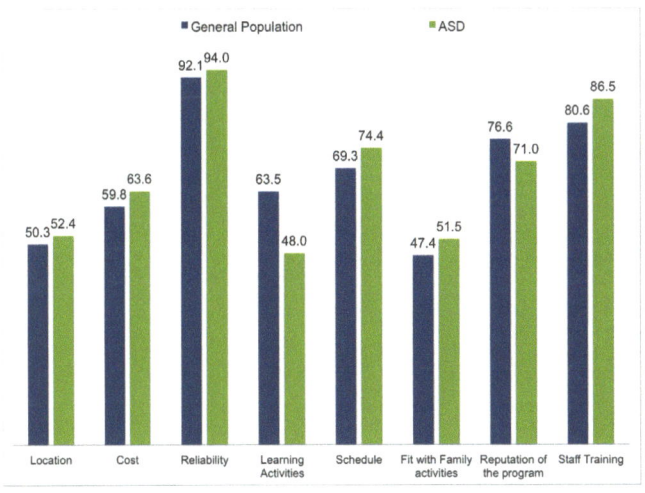

FIGURE 7. IMPORTANCE OF RATINGS OF CHILD CARE ATTRIBUTES.

Parents identified reliability, training of the staff, reputation, and schedule as the most important attributes, followed by learning activities, costs, location, and fit with other family activities. There were no statistically significant differences between families of children with ASD and the general population. There is no evidence that having a child with ASD influences parental preferences for child care attributes.

SUMMARY

This section has looked in detail at arrow 3 in the theoretical framework: do families with children with ASD prefer different attributes than other families when selecting child care? Across seven attributes, from cost and location to staff training and learning activities, there were no detectable differences in preferences.

Families with children with ASD value the same attributes in child care arrangements as other families in the United States. In particular, two-thirds or more of families in the study rated reliability, staff training, reputation, and schedule of the program as very important. Location, cost, learning activities, and the fit of the program with other family activities were rated as very important by about half to two-thirds of the sample. No attributes were considered to have little importance when making a child care decision.

These results are consistent with a number of studies from the 1990s, which found that parents place non-quality attributes above learning and quality as defined by experts (Johansen and Leibowitz 1996; Seo 2003; Zinzeleta and Little 1997). Although identification of top characteristics that influence the child care decision have been shown to vary by method of data collection (Kesinger Rose and Elicker 2008), there is no reason to believe that the method of asking the question would influence differences between the ASD group and the general population.

CHAPTER 6:
CHILD CARE ARRANGEMENTS

This chapter explores the actual child care arrangements made by families, construct G in the theoretical model.

In this study, parents were informed that by the term child care, we meant, "All types of childcare arrangements you have including before and after school activities or programs, babysitters, etc." Regular child care arrangement was defined a "regular childcare arrangement or activity, or a before or after school activity or program that they attend at least once per week."

REGULAR CHILD CARE ARRANGEMENTS

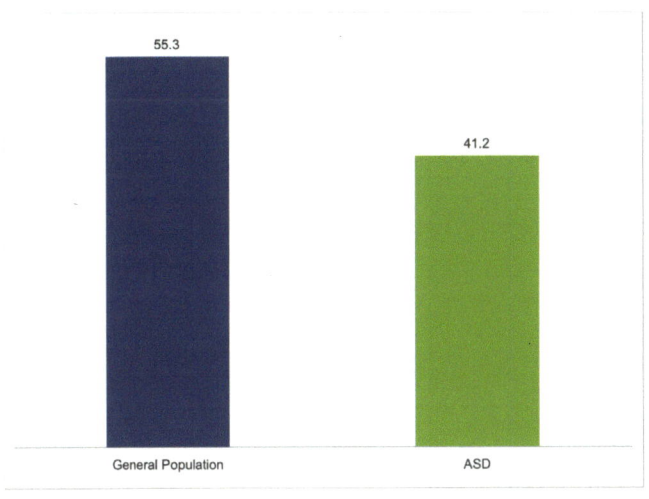

FIGURE 8. HOUSEHOLDS WITH WEEKLY CHILD CARE ARRANGEMENTS.

Compared with the general population, families of children with ASD were just as likely to have regular a child care arrangement, defined as weekly child care arrangements.

HOUSEHOLDS WITH WEEKLY CHILD CARE ARRANGEMENTS

TYPES OF CHILD CARE ARRANGEMENTS

Parents who had reported their family had a weekly child care arrangement were asked, "Please, tell me whether or not any of your children (your child) has used any of the following types of childcare or before or after school activities during this school year. How about (a) spending time with a parent or guardian who does not live in your household, (b) childcare in your home provided by a nanny or relative other than the parent or guardian, (c) using a before school program at the child's school, (d) using an after school program at the child's school, (e) attending after school activities not at the child's school, (f) some other childcare arrangement, either before or after school." Some options are not shown because they were asked of parents of children in the target age range (e.g. three- to four-year-olds for preschool), and this study had very few children with ASD in those age categories to show results. Thus, the settings in the above figure show the child care arrangements mostly for children ages five to thirteen.

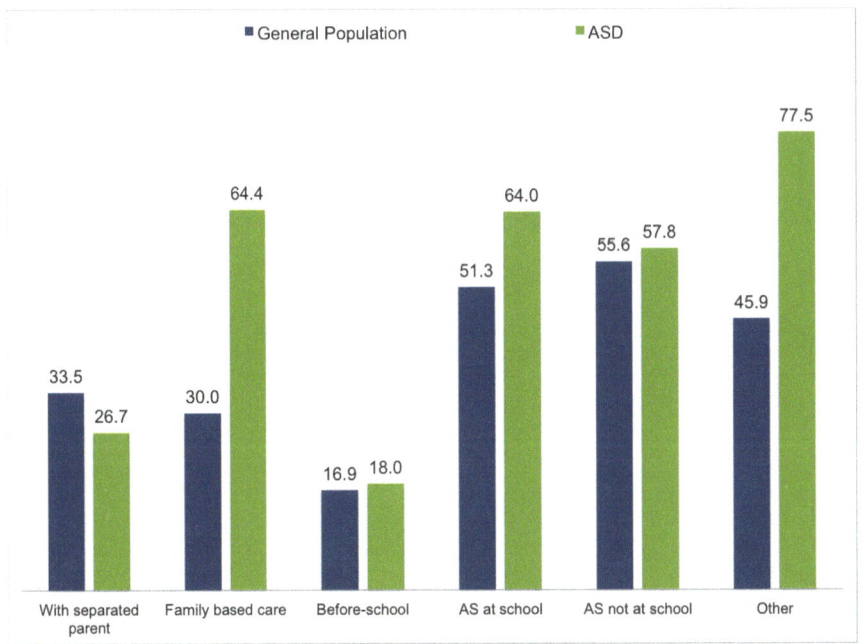

FIGURE 9. CHILD CARE SETTINGS.
NOTE: AS – AFTER SCHOOL PROGRAM OR ACTIVITY.

The only significant difference in the setting of weekly child care arrangement was higher use of the "other" arrangement by families of children with ASD (OR 4.06, p<.05).

Parents were asked if their children (child) had participated in programs that emphasized (a) music, (b) dance activities, (c) arts, (d) sports or physical activities, (e) tutoring services out of school hours, (f) training in some aspect of behavior or self-control, (g) religious groups or activities, (h) book clubs, or (i) scouts or similar groups or clubs.

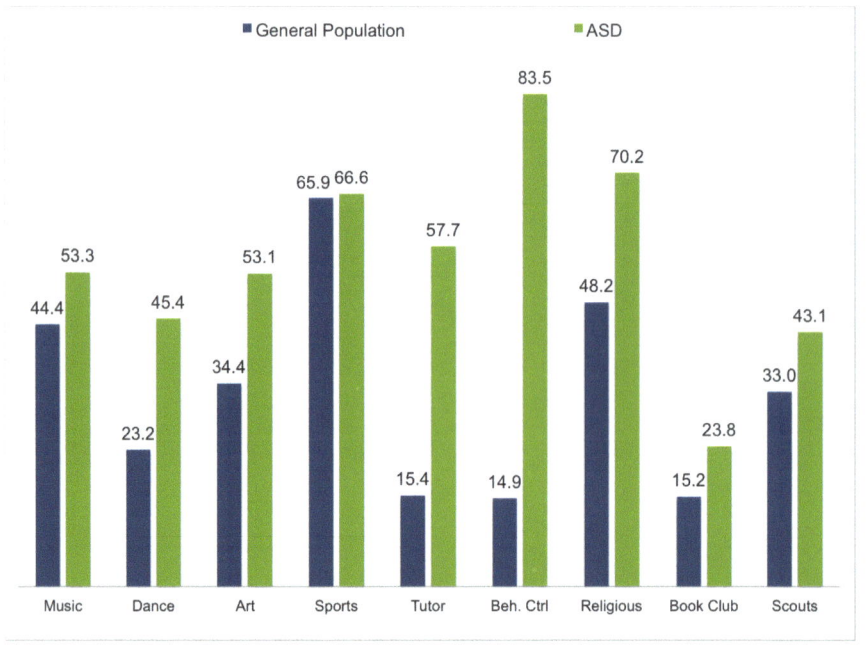

Figure 10. Content of activities.
Note: Beh. Crtl – programs with training in some aspect of behavior or self-control.

Families of children with ASD were more likely to report a weekly regular child care arrangement that included behavior training (83.5% vs. 14.9%, p<.01, OR 28.9) or tutoring (57.75 vs. 15.4%, p<.01, OR 7.49). Thus, much of what happens before and after school hours can be rightly considered additional training and learning. These do not appear to be simply leisure activities. In this study's sample, these families also attended religious activity (70.2 vs. 48.2, p>.05) and dance activities (45.4 vs. 23.3, p>.05) more frequently, but these differences were not statistically significant. Families of children with ASD were just as likely to report having weekly regular arrangements that included musical or artistic activities, participation in sports, scouts or similar groups, and book clubs. Therefore, families with children with ASD who elect to have weekly child care activities were involved in every form of community program.

NOT PARTICIPATING IN THE CHILD CARE MARKETS

About three-quarters of the families with children with ASD did not have any weekly regular child care arrangements, compared with two-thirds of the general population in our sample. From a policy perspective, it is important to know whether the decision not to use child care regularly is an expression of preference or a result of constraints in the community supply, of budget constraints, or of informational constraints.

REASONS NOT TO HAVE CHILD CARE

Parents who reported no weekly child care arrangement were asked, "Please tell me if each of the following was a major reason, a minor reason, or not a reason at all why your child/children are not enrolled in any program or childcare. Is it (a) because your children are too young, (b) because you prefer to raise your child/children yourself, (c) because your children develop best at home, (d) because you could not afford childcare, (e) because you could not arrange transportation, (f) because you could not find quality care, (g) because you could not find a program that met your child's/children's needs, (h) because your child/one or more of your children needs specialized care, or (i) some other reason." Note that some of the reasons specify preferences while others target financial, transportation, or supply constraints.

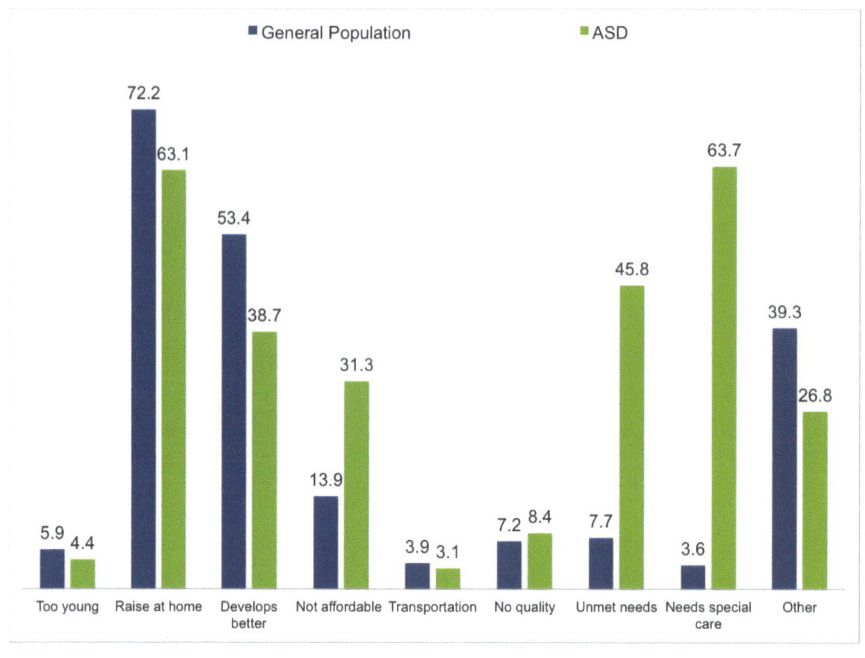

FIGURE 11. REASONS NOT TO HAVE A REGULAR CHILD CARE ARRANGEMENT.

Families with children with ASD who did not have regular child care arrangements gave similar reasons for the choice to provide care in the home: more than half stated that they simply prefer to raise their children at home. Yet, there were two statistically significant differences that expressed supply constraints. First, families with children with ASD were ten times more likely to state that the needs of their children would not be met by child care providers (45.8% vs. 7.7%, p<.01, OR 10.13), and second, corroborating the first point, they were forty-seven times more likely to report that the needs of their children would not be met (63.7% vs. 3.6%, p<.01, OR 46.9). Interestingly, although families with children with ASD were more likely cite affordability, it was marginally non-significant (31.3% vs. 13.9%, p=0.06). Thus, in contrast with other parents, families of children with ASD may be choosing not to have regular child care arrangements because the child care offerings

Chapter 6: Child Care Arrangements

simply do not meet the needs of their children, at least within the price ranges they can afford.

COMPARISON OF INDIVIDUAL CHILDREN

This subsection presents unweighted comparisons between children with ASD and other focal children.

LACK OF NEEDED SERVICES

Parents were asked if the needs of the selected child were being met with the following item: "Child is receiving all the services he or she needs." Parents could indicate this statement was true or not true for the child.

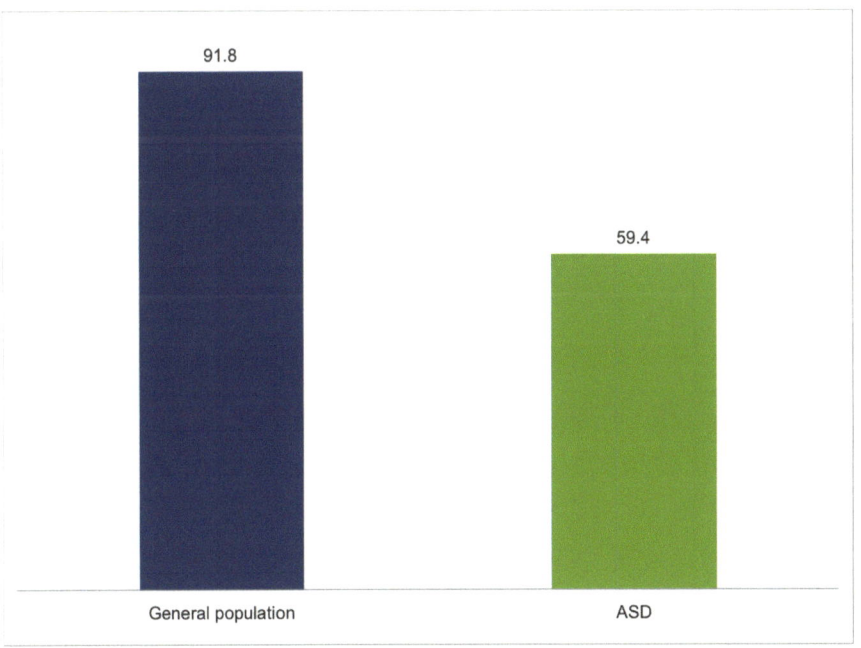

FIGURE 12. CHILD RECEIVED ALL NEEDED SERVICES.

While nine in ten children in the general population received all needed services, only six in ten children with ASD received what they needed (59.4% vs. 91.8%, p<.01, OR 0.13).

RESPONSE FROM SYSTEMS TO CHILD'S BEHAVIOR

Parents were asked if the following statements were true or not for the focal child: "(a) child was expelled or asked not to return from a child care arrangement because of behavior problems, (b) child was suspended or expelled from school or child care."

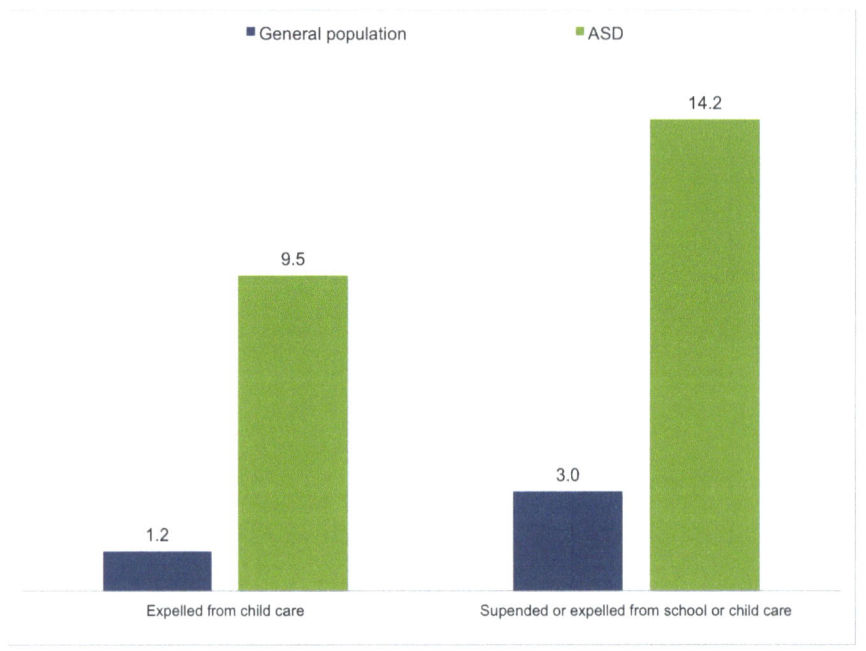

FIGURE 13. EXPULSIONS AND SUSPENSIONS FROM CHILD CARE AND SCHOOL.

Parents reported high levels of expulsion for children with ASD. One in ten children with ASD was reported to have been expelled or asked not to return to a child care arrangement (9.5% vs. 1.2%, p<.01, OR 8.6). In addition, children with ASD were expelled or suspended in school or child care settings at much higher rates than the general population (14.2% vs. 3%, p<.01, OR 5.4)

VICTIMIZATION BY BULLYING AND RECEIVING IMPROPER TREATMENT

Parents were asked if the following statements regarding their selected child receiving maltreatment by peers or adults in school and child care settings were true or not true: "(a) child was bullied at a school or child care setting and (b) child was not properly treated by staff at a school or child care setting."

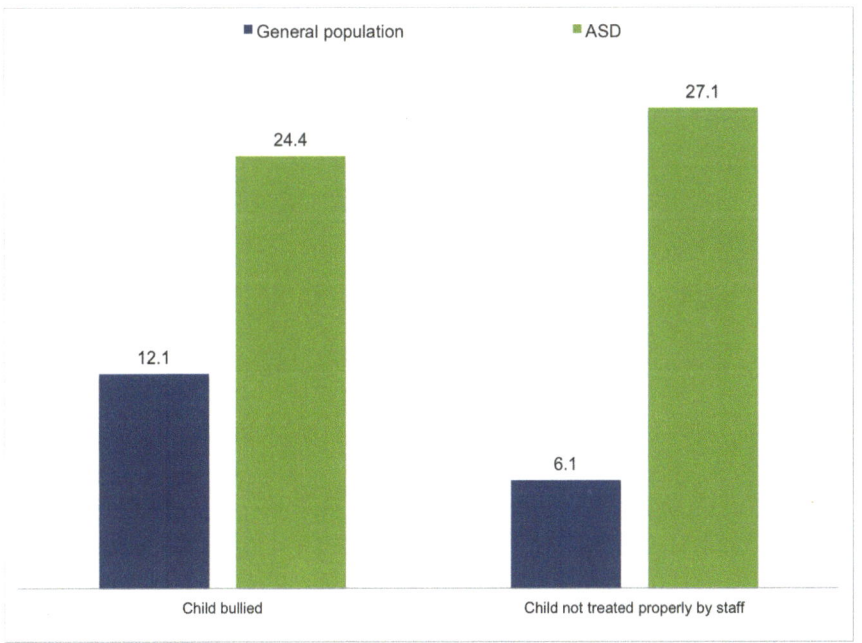

FIGURE 14. VICTIMIZATION BY PEERS AND IMPROPER TREATMENT BY STAFF.

Children with ASD had double the odds of being victimized by bullies at school or in child care (24.4% vs. 12.1%, p<.05, OR 2.3). Even worse, children with ASD were more likely to be improperly treated by school or child care staff than children in the general population (27.1% vs. 6.1%, p<.01, OR 5.7).

SUMMARY

In our sample, about one-quarter of families with children with ASD had regular child care arrangements, a comparable percentage with the one-third in the general population. Those who participate, however, were as likely, if not more, to participate in many community and school-based programs that involved a variety of diverse artistic, athletic, and educational activities. Thus, schools and community providers must anticipate the need to welcome families of children with ASD into their programs and activities.

Families of children with ASD reported higher use of programs that offered tutoring or had a behavior training component. This finding raises the issue of whether children with ASD have sufficient play time, as well as whether the regular school year and school hours are sufficient to meet their academic needs.

In addition, we found that children with ASD had much higher rates of victimization, were more likely to be improperly treated by staff, and were more likely to be suspended and expelled from child care or school or both. While some of these findings corroborate previous research on expulsions for preschool-age children with behavior problems (Gilliam and Shahar 2006), our sample is mostly school-age children. Thus, concern about the care these children receive in child care and school is warranted.

CHAPTER 7:
BUDGET CONSTRAINT INFORMATION

This chapter explores evidence of financial constraints on child care decision-making, an important part of construct E in the theoretical model.

An important issue for policymakers is to distinguish between child care choices that are an expression of preference and those that are caused by binding constraints. To partially address this issue, we asked families who had regular child care arrangements and families who did not if they would have made the same child care choices or made the choice not to have regular weekly child care arrangements had their income doubled. An affirmative response would indicate that a substantial expansion of the budget constraint would have no impact on the decision, thus indicating the constraint was not binding.

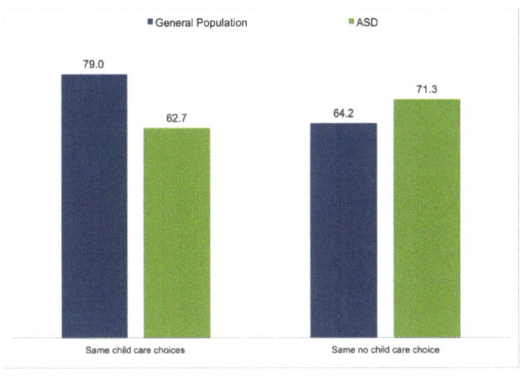

FIGURE 15. WOULD HAVE MADE SAME CHILD CARE CHOICES IF INCOME DOUBLED.

About three in four families in the general population who had regular child care arrangements informed us that if their income had doubled they would have made the same choices, thus suggesting that the income constraint was not binding. Among the families in the general population who did not report a regular child care arrangement, about three in five estimated that they would make no changes in their decision not to have a regular child care arrangement if their income doubled. Families of children with ASD did not differ significantly from the general population.

DIFFICULTY PAYING FOR CHILD CARE

Parents who chose weekly child care arrangements were asked, "How easy it is for you to pay these childcare costs? Would you say very easy, somewhat easy, somewhat difficult, or very difficult?" If the parent responded, "somewhat" or "very difficult," it was coded as a household that had difficulty paying for child care costs.

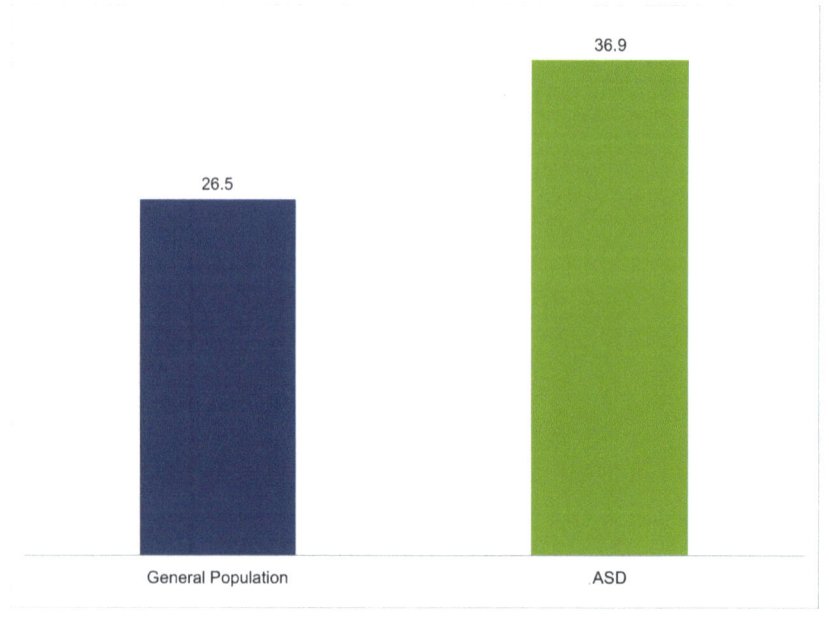

FIGURE 16. DIFFICULTY PAYING FOR CHILD CARE.

Families of children with ASD were more likely to report having difficulty paying for child care expenses than was the general population (36.9% vs. 26.5%, p<.05, OR 1.6).

SUMMARY

The majority of American families reported no binding budget constraints by indicating that their child care choices would not be modified by a doubling of their income. Families with children with ASD were similar, with roughly two-thirds reporting no anticipated changes to child care arrangements, including the decision of not using a weekly child care arrangement, if their income doubled.

Families with ASD, however, indicated greater difficulty paying for child care.

CHAPTER 8:
ASSESSING THE SUPPLY OF CHILD CARE

This chapter explores the community supply of child care, construct F in the theoretical model.

Parents were asked to rate the supply of different types of child care in their communities as excellent, good, fair, or poor. Eight types of care were rated: (a) infant-toddler care, (b) preschool, (c) before school care, (d) after school care, (e) care during the evenings, (f) care for children with special needs, (g) care during weekends, and (h) affordable care.

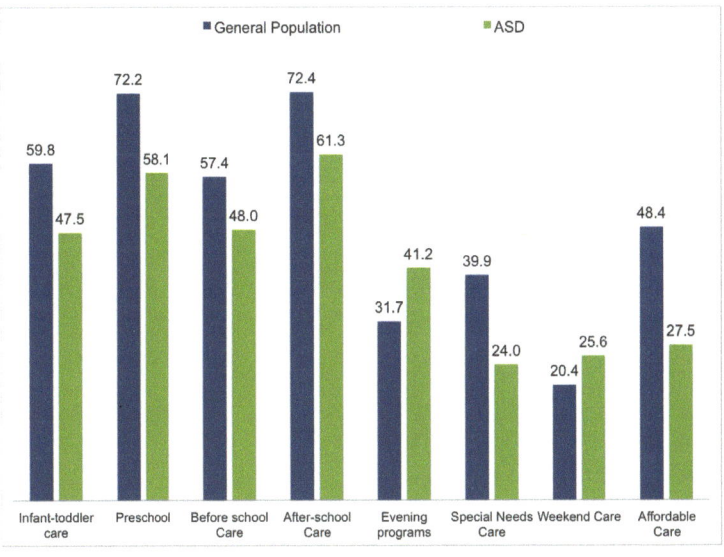

FIGURE 17. SUPPLY OF CHILD CARE IN THE COMMUNITY.

Parents of children with ASD rated the supply of child care in their communities similarly to parents in the general population. After school care, prekindergarten, and infant/toddler care were more likely to be rated good or excellent than evening or weekend care, or care for children with special needs. Families with children with ASD were less likely to rate good or excellent the supply of affordable care in their communities (27.5% vs. 48.4%, p<.05, OR 0.4).

CHAPTER 9: UNMET CHILD CARE NEEDS

This chapter explores the level of unmet child care needs. Unmet child care needs were represented by construct H in the theoretical model of Chapter 3.

UNMET CHILD CARE NEEDS

As a measure of unmet child care needs, parents were asked the following yes/no question: "Since the beginning of the school year, did your family have any times when you needed childcare but you were unable to get it?" Similarly, as a measure of unmet needs for respite care, parents were asked the yes/no question, "Does your family have a need for respite care, including more babysitters, so that you (or your spouse or partner) have some time off from your caregiving responsibilities?"

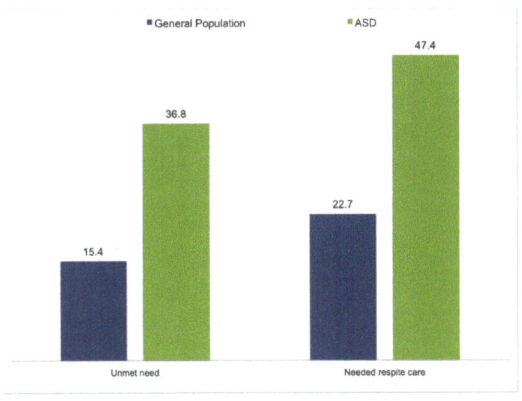

FIGURE 18. UNMET CHILD CARE NEEDS AND NEEDS FOR RESPITE CARE.

About one-third of families with children with ASD reported having this type of unmet child care need, compared to one-sixth of families in the general population (36.8% vs. 15.4%, p<.01, OR 3.2). Thus, families with children with ASD were three times as likely to have unmet child care needs.

Respite care is normally understood as substitute care to allow the primary caregiver some needed free time and to prevent caregiver burnout. Families with children with ASD were three times as likely to report they needed respite care (47.4% vs. 22.7%, p<.01, OR 3.1). Almost half of the families with children with ASD reported needing respite care, and about one in five of families of children without ASD reported the need as well, showing that the need for respite care affects millions of U.S. households.

LAST-MINUTE CHILD CARE ARRANGEMENTS

Another approach we took to the issue of unmet child care needs was to measure the number of last-minute child care arrangements the family had to make due to unforeseen circumstances. We used a question previously used in the National Survey of Children's Health, 2003.

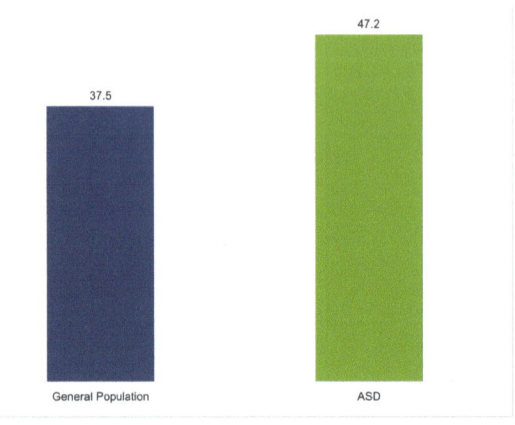

FIGURE 19. MADE LAST-MINUTE ARRANGEMENTS IN THE LAST MONTH.

By this measure, 37.5% of the general population and 47.2% of the families with children with ASD had to make last-minute child care arrangements during the past month because of circumstances beyond their control. The difference was not statistically significant.

A SIGN OF DIFFICULT CHOICES: LEAVING CHILDREN BEHIND

As a measure of the difficult compromises families face when choosing between work and home obligations, parents were asked, "In the last three months, have you (or your spouse or partner) felt you should stay home with your child/children but went to work anyway because you were worried about the impact on your job?"

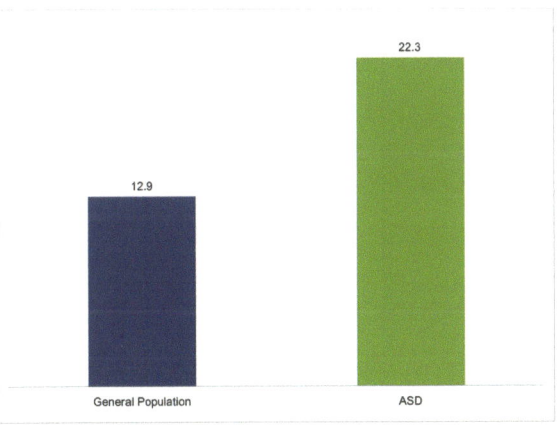

FIGURE 20. WENT TO WORK WHEN SHOULD HAVE STAYED WITH CHILD.

About one in ten families in the general population reported having made this choice, compared with one in five families with children with ASD. The difference was not statistically significant (22.3% vs. 12.9%, p>.05).

PERSISTENT CONCERNS ABOUT CHILD CARE

Another way to investigate the issue of unmet child care needs is to ask parents who use child care services about their persistent concerns. Parents who used weekly child care were asked, "Since the beginning of the school year, have you been repeatedly concerned about any of the following issues regarding your child's (any of your children's) childcare? How about (a) safety, (b) untrained staff, (c) your child's developmental needs are not met, (d) negative influence from peers, (e) lack of reliability, and (f) cost?" Parents could answer either yes or no.

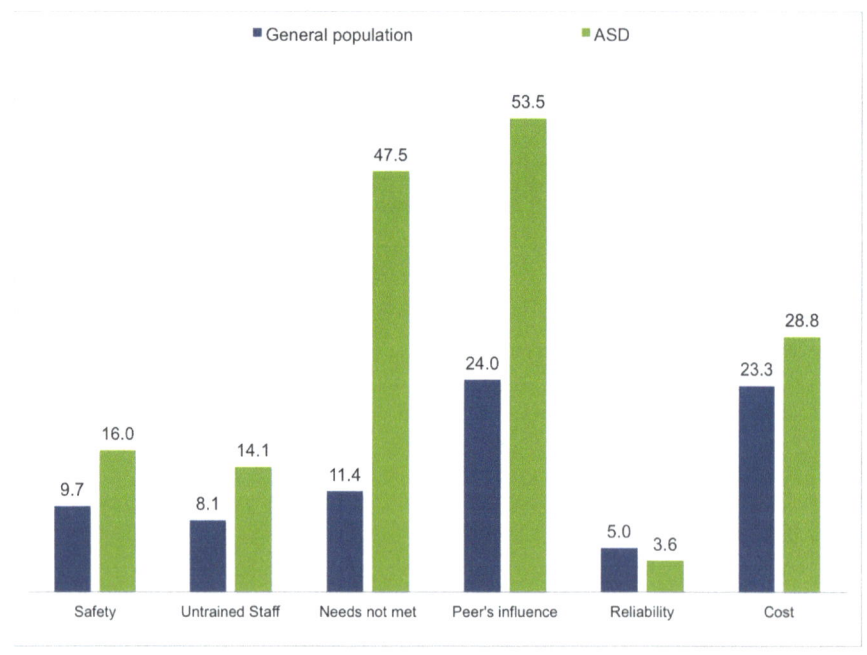

FIGURE 21. PERSISTENT CONCERNS ABOUT CHILD CARE.

Parents of children with ASD were concerned repeatedly about their children's developmental needs not being met in the child care setting (47.5% vs. 11.4%, p<.01, OR 7.0) and the negative influence of peers on their children (53.5% vs. 24.0%, p<.05, OR 3.6).

SUMMARY

The answers to these questions reveal a complex reality: (a) families with children with ASD are three times more likely to report they need child care and do not have it, although (b) it affects only one-third of the families with ASD; and (c) about one-half of the families needed to make at least one last-minute child care arrangement in the previous thirty days. Thus, the problem of unmet child care needs may be related to finding the right care and keeping it.

Parents of children with ASD who used weekly child care arrangements reported repeated concerns about the influence of peers and whether their children's developmental needs were met. These concerns corroborate previous findings on peer victimization and potential for maltreatment by staff in Chapter 6.

CHAPTER 10:
IMPACT OF UNMET CHILD CARE NEEDS ON THE FAMILY

In this chapter, we report the changes in employment that parents attribute to child care problems, as well as indicators on their parenting (construct I and arrow 9). The chapter also discusses child care-related parental stress, construct J, and other impacts on parenting.

EMPLOYMENT STATUS

Households in America are enormously dynamic in the type and variety of employment combinations they have. Parents were asked, "Now, we would like to understand your current employment situation in the household. Are any of the following statements true for you (or your spouse or partner)?" The figures report the percentage of households that answered affirmatively for either one or both parents.

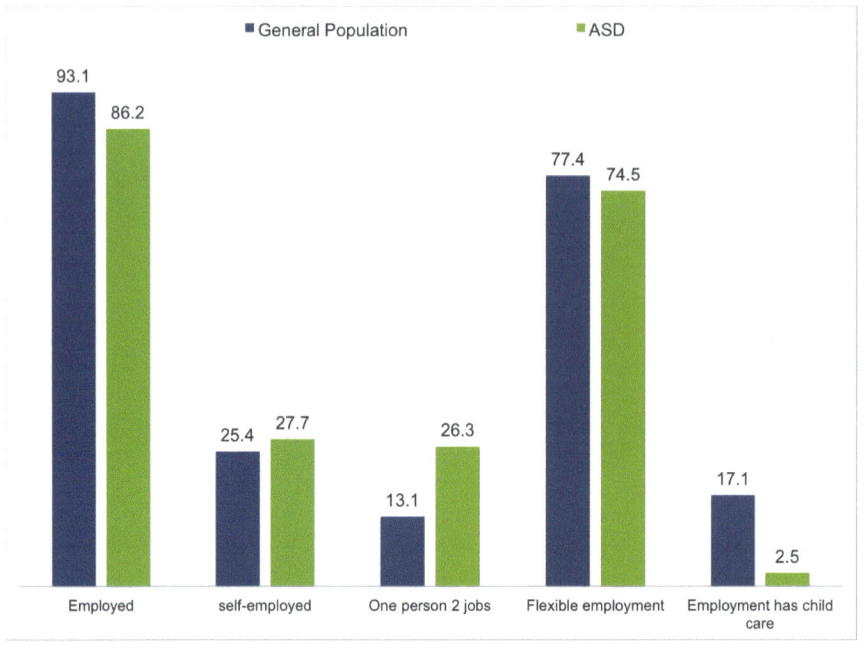

FIGURE 22. EMPLOYMENT ARRANGEMENTS.

As reported before, the vast majority of households in our sample were employed; about one-quarter reported self-employment. Importantly, three-quarters of the households in both groups reported having flexible employment. Parents of children with ASD were more likely to report that one parent had two jobs (26.3% vs. 13.1, p<.05, OR 2.4) and that their employment did not provide child care benefits (2.5% vs. 17.1%, p<.01, OR 0.1).

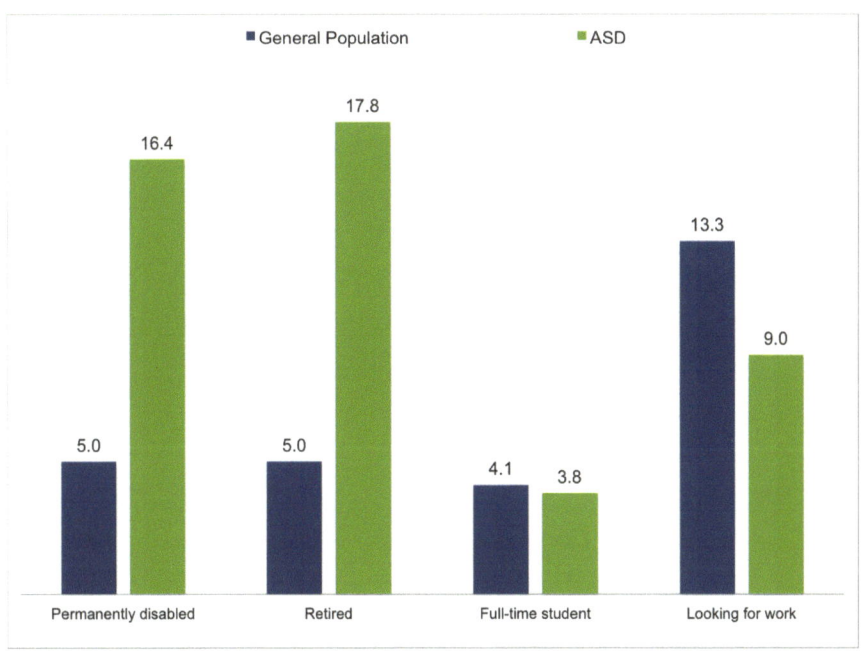

FIGURE 23. OTHER OCCUPATIONAL VARIABLES.

Regarding other occupational variables, parents of children with ASD reported that they were more likely to be retired (17.8% vs. 5%, p<.05, OR 4.1) or permanently disabled (16.4% vs. 5%, p<.05, OR 3.7) than parents of other households, while the likelihood of the parents pursuing studies full-time or looking for work was comparable to the general population.

CHILD CARE-INDUCED CHANGES IN EMPLOYMENT

Previous research documented unmet child care needs and lower levels of parental employment and inferred that child care problems were the cause of employment problems. We find such an approach problematic because households change employment conditions for a large variety of reasons. Thus, many parents in households with child care needs may change employment because of non-child care-related factors. In this study, we asked parents to report only the changes they attribute to child care problems. Parents were asked directly to tell us if any of following nine types of employment changes *were caused by child care problems* (of any child in the household). The nine changes were: (a) quit a job, (b) been absent from work, (c) decreased job performance, (d) changed a work schedule, (e) looked for a different job, (f) modified a current job substantially, (g) turned down a job, (h) stopped looking for work, or (i) made decisions that negatively impact future employability.

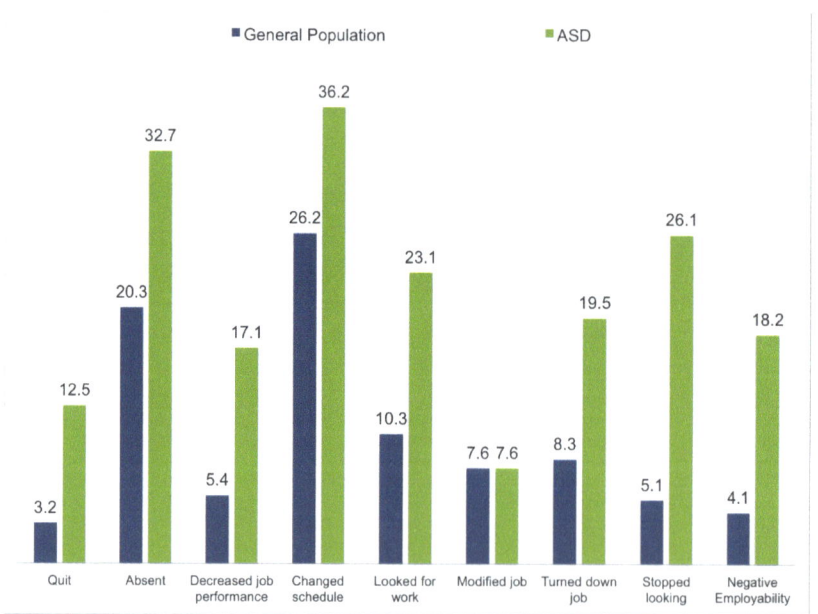

FIGURE 24. CHILD CARE IMPACTS ON EMPLOYMENT.

Families with children with ASD were more likely to report that child care problems had resulted in quitting a job (12.5 vs. 3.2, p<.05, OR 4.3), decreased job performance (17.1 vs. 5.4, p<.05, OR 3.6), looking for another job (23.1 vs. 10.3, p<.05, OR 2.6), turning down a job offer (19.5 vs. 8.3, p<.01, OR 2.7), stopping looking for work (26.1 vs. 5.1, p<.01, OR 6.6), and making decisions that impact future employability negatively (18.2 vs. 4.1, p<.01, OR 5.2).

There were no significant differences for reporting absenteeism, changes in work schedule, and having modified job substantially as a result of child care problems. Therefore, families with children with ASD are at significantly higher risk of reporting that child care problems led to substantial changes in employment, particularly for the gravest changes such as quitting a job, leaving the workforce, and making decisions that will impact future employability negatively.

Overall, about two-thirds of the families with children with ASD reported that child care problems had at least one of these impacts (68.3 vs. 45.6, p<.01). Given that changing work schedule and modifying current employment arrangement were the most common responses in the population to child care problems, we also calculated the probability that families of children with ASD had the less common child care-related employment impacts and found that the majority of families reported these more severe impacts compared with one-quarter of the general population (50.5 vs. 24.1, p<.01).

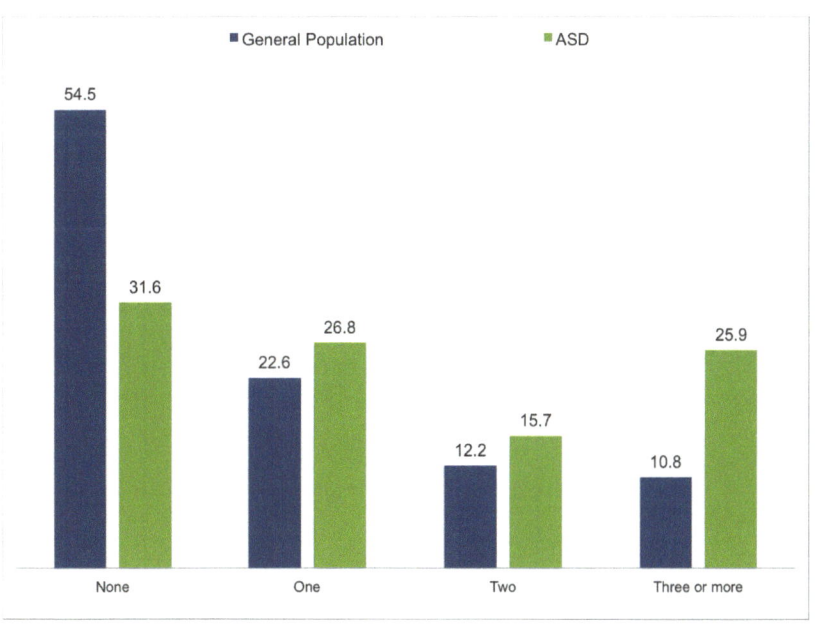

FIGURE 25. NUMBER OF EMPLOYMENT CHANGES DUE TO CHILD CARE PROBLEMS.

Of course, child care problems can result in multiple employment changes. By this standard, families of children with ASD also fared comparatively worse. They were much more likely than the general population to report three or more child care-caused employment changes (25.9 vs. 10.8 p<.01).

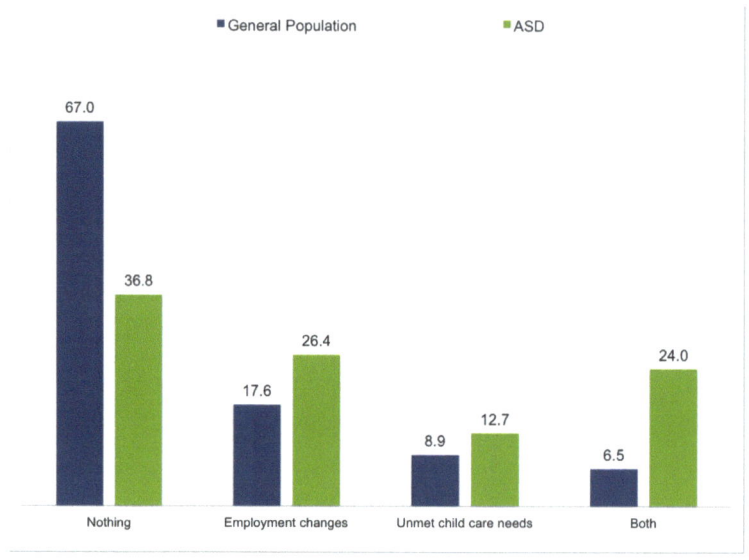

FIGURE 26. RELATIONSHIP BETWEEN UNMET CHILD CARE NEEDS AND CHILD CARE IMPACTS ON EMPLOYMENT.

Not surprisingly, families with children with ASD were more likely to report both unmet child care needs and that employment was impacted by child care problems (24 vs. 6.5, p<.05, OR 4.5).

CHILD CARE-INDUCED PARENTAL STRESS

Respondents were asked, "Since the beginning of the school year, have you (or your spouse or partner) had high, medium, low, or no stress at work because of problems with childcare?" Child care-related stress at home was measured with an identical question that changed the words "at work" for "at home."

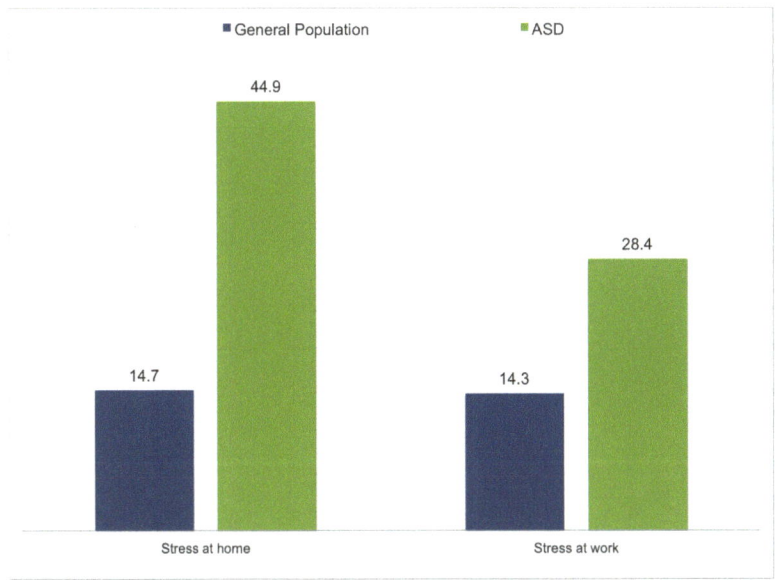

FIGURE 27. CHILD CARE-RELATED STRESS AT HOME AND AT WORK.

Families with children with ASD were twice as likely to report medium or high stress at work because of child care problems (28.4% vs. 14.3%, p<.05, OR 2.4) than the general population. They were almost five times more likely to report child care-related parental stress at home (44.9% vs. 14.7%, p<.01, OR 4.7). Interestingly, while in the general population the level of child care-related stress is similar at work and at home, for families with children with ASD, the stress was more likely to be higher in both settings but was most frequently reported at home.

PARENTING

Parents were asked three questions to measure various aspects related to parenting. First, we had a measure of emotional support with parenting: "Is there someone that you can turn to for day-to-day emotional help with raising children? (yes/no)." As a rough measure of parent self-efficacy, parents were also asked, "In general, how well do you feel you are coping with the day-to-day demands of raising children? Would you say that you are coping (a) very well, (b) somewhat well, (c) not very well, or (d) not well at all." The survey also asked parents, "Since the beginning of the school year, how would you rate how you (or spouse or partner) balance work and family responsibilities? Would you say (a) excellent, (b) good, (c) fair, or (d) poor?"

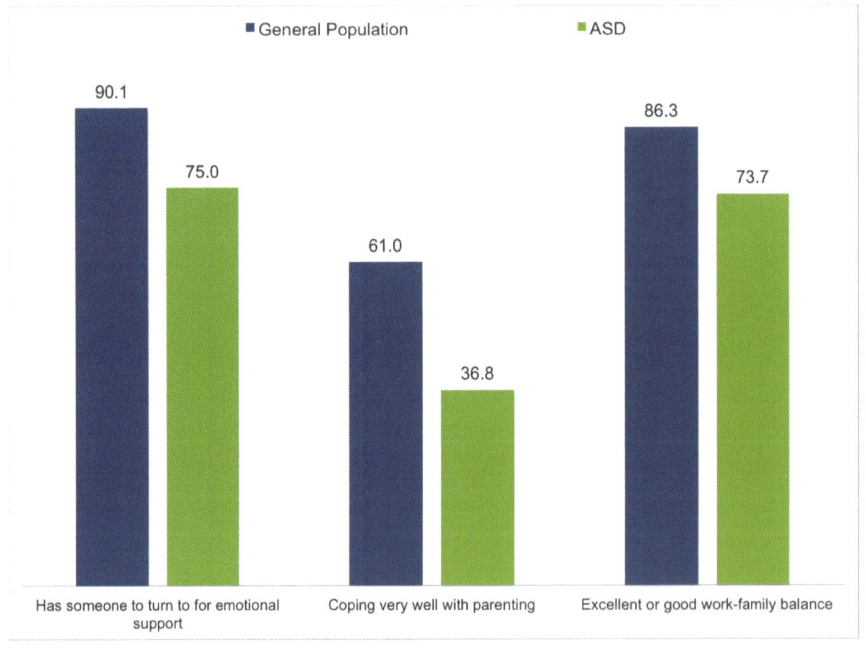

FIGURE 28. PARENTING VARIABLES.

Thirty-six percent of parents of children with ASD reported coping very well with the parenting role, compared with 61% in the general population (p<.01, OR 0.4). Twenty-five percent of families with children with ASD reported having no one to turn for parenting support, compared with 9.9% for the general population (p<.01, OR 0.3). Finally, 74% of families with children with ASD reported good or excellent family-work balance, compared with 86% in the general population, a finding that was marginally non-significant (p=.05).

Thus, across the board, parents of children with ASD reported lower self-efficacy and emotional support. Of particular concern is that two-thirds of parents of children with ASD reported not coping very well with parenting.

SOURCES OF PARENTAL ADVICE

Parents were asked, "When you need important advice on parenting, who do you primarily go to? (a) The child's pediatrician, (b) the child's teacher, (c) friends, (d) family, (e) the Internet, (f) mental health (MH) professional, (g) others (e.g. work, church, etc.) or (h) no one?"

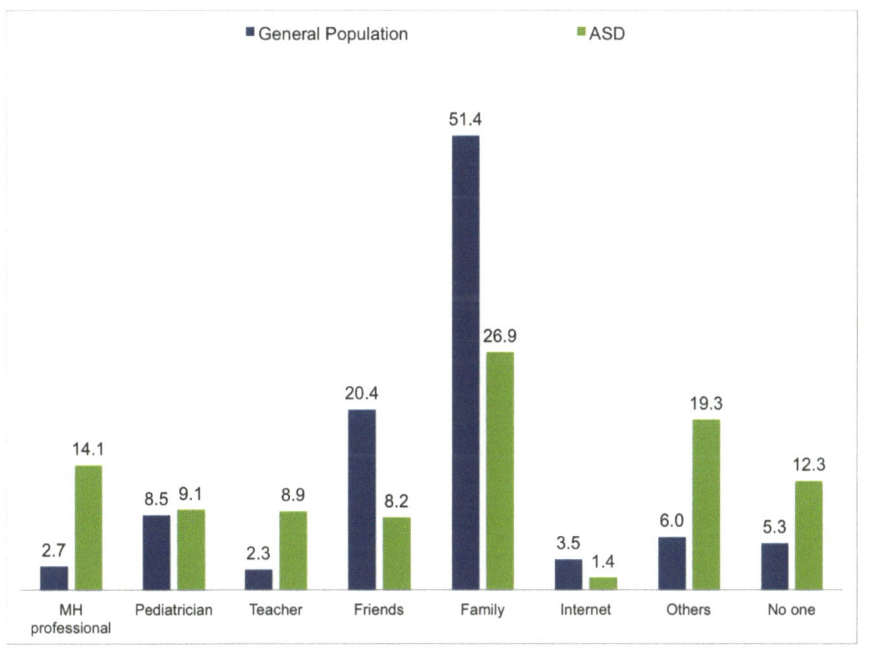

FIGURE 29. PRIMARY SOURCE OF PARENTING ADVICE.
NOTE: MH – MENTAL HEALTH.

Families with children with ASD were less likely to rely on families, friends, or the Internet for important parenting advice; they were more likely to rely on mental health professionals, teachers, and others (e.g. work, church, etc.). A little more than one in ten households with children with ASD reported not having any source for important parenting advice, compared with one in twenty for the general population.

PARENTAL ILLNESS

Parenting stress can result in a number of illnesses, and conversely a number of ailments can make parenting difficult and contribute to stress. There have been many studies reporting that mothers of children with ASD are at higher risk of depression or anxiety, although some studies have also shown that mothers manage quite well with a child who may be more challenging to parent. In our study, we asked, "During the last twelve months, has a doctor or health professional told a parent in the household that he or she has any of the following conditions: (a) clinical depression, (b) anxiety disorder, (c) any stress-induced condition?" A fourth category, serious illness, was not reported for any parent of a child with ASD and is not reported below. The respondent could indicate "Yes, myself; yes, spouse or partner; yes, both; or no, neither." Because of our low sample, we report any parental illness versus none.

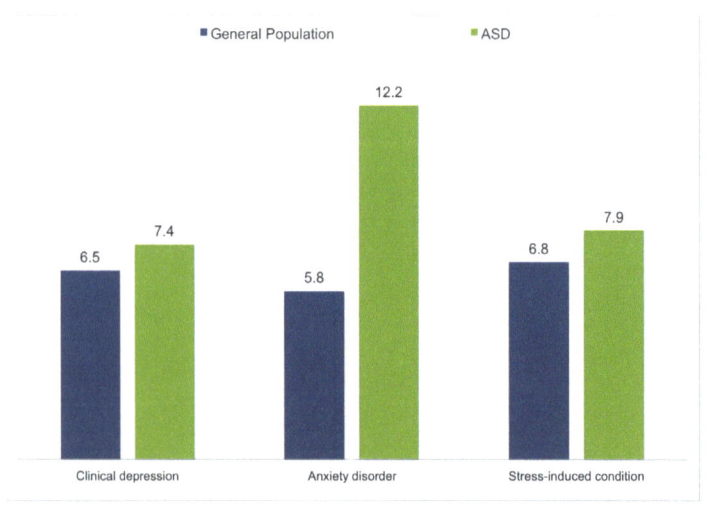

Figure 30. Parental illness in the last twelve months.

There were no statistically significant differences between parents of children with ASD and other parents in clinical depression, anxiety disorders or stress-induced conditions. Anxiety disorders were non-significantly higher (12.2% vs. 5.8%, p>.05).

SUMMARY

It is apparent that families with children with ASD are like other families in that they try to compensate for child care problems by changing work schedules and being absent from work. They use these strategies more in our sample, but the difference is not statistically significant. Yet, these strategies are not enough, and, thus, families with children with ASD resort to less frequent and more severe remedies to achieve work-family balance, such as making decisions that impact future employability negatively, quitting jobs, and turning down offers of employment. The differences here are statistically significant at the 5% or 1% level even though our sample is quite small.

Importantly, around two-thirds of families with children with ASD report these impacts of unmet child care needs on their employment status. This research elucidates previous work documenting that families with children with ASD experience substantial earning losses (Montes and Halterman 2008). Clearly, if families with children with ASD are more likely to report more severe, and more frequent, child care impacts on employment than other families, that would be a reason their earning suffers.

Additionally, child care problems take a nonfinancial toll. Between one-quarter and one-half of families of children with ASD report child care-induced stress at home and at work. Less than half report coping very well with the parenting role, compared with two-thirds for the general population. Finally, they are also more likely to report having less emotional support, and one in ten families reported having no primary source for any parenting advice.

Child care needs are not only unmet, they are also having profound consequences on the lives of these families.

CHAPTER 11: WHAT HAVE WE LEARNED

MAIN FINDINGS OF THE STUDY

This study is the most comprehensive exploration of the child care situation for households with children with ASD in the United States. Although our focus was ages zero to thirteen, most of the children with ASD were school age. There are four major themes:

(1) **Families of children with ASD are much like other families.** Families of children with autism spectrum disorders (ASD) are very much like other families in a number of factors thought to influence the child care decision making process. In particular, families of children with ASD receive child care services in every community setting and offering. All sectors that offer activities for children, including the religious sector, family care, center care, and tutoring services can expect to come in contact with families of children with ASD.

Like other families, families of children with ASD have strong preferences for well-respected programs that offer engaging learning activities in accessible places at prices they can afford. Like many other families, they have adjusted or modified their employment to meet their child care needs. Those families that decided not to use child care on a regular basis and have a child with ASD give many of the same reasons for their decision that other families in similar situations give. Finally, families of children with ASD were similar in terms of annual income, education, race, and other similar demographic characteristics (see Table 1).

(2) **Families of children with ASD report much higher levels of unmet need.** There were some very notable differences between the child care experiences of families of children with ASD and other families. Compared with other families, families of children with ASD were three times more likely to report unmet child care needs and needing respite care, eight times more likely to report their children were not receiving all needed services, eight times more likely to report their children were expelled from child care, and five times more likely to report their children were suspended or expelled from schools. When they used child care, they were seven times more likely to have persistent concerns that their children's needs were not being met, and four times more likely to be persistently concerned about negative peer influences.

In some cases, the decision not to use child care was heavily constrained by unavailable supply. Families of children with ASD were ten times more likely to report not using child care because it would not meet their children's needs, and forty-seven times more likely to cite their children's special needs as a reason not to have a weekly child care arrangement. They were eight times less likely to have employment that provided child care.

(3) **Families with ASD are more likely to report child care problems that impact employment.** Compared with other families, families with children with ASD were three times more likely to report that child care problems had resulted in decreased job performance, looking for new jobs, and turning down job offers. They were four times more likely to report

quitting a job because of child care problems. They were five times more likely to report having made employment decisions that negatively impact future employability, and six times more likely to report having stopped looking for work because of child care problems. They were twice as likely to report three or more child care-related employment impacts, and four times as likely to report both unmet child care needs and child care-related employment impacts compared to other families. They were twice as likely as other families to report that an adult in the household had two jobs.

(4) **Families with children with ASD were more likely to report child care-related high stress** both at home and at work; they were three times more likely to report they had no one to turn to for emotional support, and twice as likely to report not coping well with their parenting role. They were twice as likely to report not using family as a source of parenting advice, and five times more likely to report using mental health professionals as a source of parenting advice.

There are several key conclusions:

(1) **Every community setting that offers activities for children, including religious institutions, dance academies, family child care, tutoring services, and center child care programs, should expect and be prepared to care for children with ASD and their siblings.** Currently, preparations have focused on preparing school settings, particularly at younger ages, to receive children with ASD. It appears that no systematic training or preparation in other settings is occurring. Further, no preparation at all is occurring to accommodate siblings of children with ASD, who present with their own set of issues (Bagenholm and Gillberg 1991; Gold 1993; Mates 1990; Macks and Reeve 2007).

(2) **Families are constrained by a scarce supply of trained caregivers.** Families with ASD reported not participating in care because they could not find affordable care that would meet their children's needs. Families of children with ASD who used care reported being concerned with their child's needs being met. In addition, in this study of child care for mostly school-age children, families of children with ASD were more likely to report expulsions, bullying, and improper treatment by staff. Clearly, there is scarcity of safe care that meets the needs of children with ASD.

(3) **Families of children with ASD report difficulty paying for child care.** In the context of other research studies showing the impact that having a child with ASD has on family finances, there is little doubt that the typical family of a child with ASD needs financial assistance.

(4) **Families of children with ASD need child care assistance to establish and maintain stable employment.** They are not only more likely to have unmet child care needs, but those unmet needs are more likely to cause multiple, severe impacts on their employment.

(5) **No limitations on parental choice are warranted** because parents of children with ASD want for their children what other parents want for their children. They want full participation in the community, and they look for care within the same child care and activity choices that are available to the rest of the American population.

DIRECTIONS FOR FUTURE RESEARCH IN THE CONTEXT OF THE IACC

In 2006, the U.S. Congress established the Interagency Autism Coordinating Committee (IACC) in the Combating Autism Act as an advisory organ to the Secretary of Health and Human Services concerning ASD research and services. The IACC is mandated to develop a strategic plan annually for federally funded ASD research.

The most current plan (2010 as of this writing), however, was silent on child care issues. This silence is troubling for three reasons: first, the Child Care Bureau is part of the U.S. Department of Health and Human Services and administers the CCDF; second, this report shows that families of children with ASD have important child care needs that are under-researched and largely unaddressed by any coordinated policy initiative; and finally, the IACC 2010 strategic report does not mention any member of the Child Care Bureau in its roster of members (Interagency Autism Coordinating Committee 2010). It appears that child care issues for families of children with ASD were simply not considered by the IACC. We could not help but notice that the roster also failed to include any representation from the U.S. Department of Education. Perhaps these omissions signal agency turfs, but given that children with ASD spend much time in three settings—home, school, and child care—one wonders whether the treatment approaches supported by the IACC primarily focusing on medical and pharmacological approaches would really meet the needs of children with ASD in all three of those settings.

Consequently, my recommendations for the IACC are:

(a) To include a member of the Child Care Bureau in future IACC strategic planning rosters to ensure coordination between child care and autism research, as well as to provide context for future federal policies both in ASD and child care.

(b) To call for research that develops effective, community-based interventions for children with

ASD in child care or community settings, particularly in light of the geographically disaggregated nature of ASD prevalence and the global trend for inclusion of children with special needs in all community settings. Any approach that makes community child care settings more able to welcome and work with children with ASD will reduce the level of unmet child care needs, lead to families facing a less constrained supply of child care establishments, and improve the prospects for more stable and better paying parental employment. However, it is unrealistic to expect the child care settings to develop these new models themselves that effectively address the behavioral, cognitive, and affective needs of children with ASD. The government has a role to play in funding the development of such models.

DIRECTIONS FOR FUTURE RESEARCH

We need additional, supplementary approaches to give us a more complete picture about the challenges of securing good child care for children with ASD. In particular, there is a need for qualitative, ethnographic studies to describe in detail the experience of families with children with ASD, the problems they encounter, the support they receive, and what is helpful and what is not.

Additionally, we need a better understanding of how parents make child care decisions. Tests of the integrative accommodation model for the general population and for parents of children with special needs are needed.

This study has shown that families with children with ASD encounter substantial employment impacts of unmet child care needs. We do not know if parents of children with ASD take advantage of national policies designed to assist with these issues, such as the Family Medical Leave Act. Although I suspect this is not the case, based on the underutilization of the FMLA generally, research is needed to determine what policies are actually helpful to families with children with ASD.

Finally, we need studies about the implementations of different policy efforts for training and support of ASD children in different settings. While we know little about how effective these trainings are for school personnel, we know next to nothing about whether training of community workers is actually effective.

METHODOLOGICAL LESSONS

To the best of my knowledge, this was the first study on child care choices made by families of school-age children with autism spectrum disorders on a population basis. Thus, it is not surprising that some methodologies worked well and others could be improved. It was very useful to have an identical questionnaire for parents of children with and without ASD. Most of the information collected can only be meaningfully interpreted by looking at similar data in the general U.S. population. Indeed, one of the major themes of this study is that families of children with ASD are in many ways just typical American families.

However, as a suggestion for future studies, two components could be added that, in retrospect, were missing: (a) a qualitative study of randomly selected group of parents of children with ASD and parents of normally developing children, to provide much needed depth about what these differential patterns in the data really mean, and (b) some sort of more formal comparison with families of children with other disabilities. Some of the formal comparison information could be extracted from the data already collected, but such analysis is beyond the scope of this project.

LIMITATIONS OF THE STUDY

This study has a number of potential limitations. All the information presented is the result of a parent survey. Some children may be undiagnosed or improperly diagnosed. Attrition, eligibility, the use of cell phones, and consent may have biased this study toward a more educated, wealthier subpopulation. If this is the case, the results likely underestimate the size of the problem.

CHAPTER 12:
DEVELOPING SUGGESTED POLICY STRATEGIES

The process to develop suggested policy strategies at the national level consisted of three phases: an analysis of how child care policy has been enacted and implemented in the United States, an analysis of parental reaction to child care policy and other relevant legislation, and the development of strategies consistent with some basic fundamental values. These values are (1) the dignity of the child with ASD, (2) subsidiarity with the family, (3) solidarity with those who face stronger constraints on their child care decision-making, and (4) the likely effectiveness of the proposed strategy within the U.S. welfare state model policy context.

My approach was to view child care policy within the liberal welfare implementation of the United States. The international perspective is needed to understand why some child care policies that flourish elsewhere languish in the United States and vice versa. Policy strategies are context dependent and would be quite different for a country like Spain, Germany, or Sweden than for the United States. Thus, in addition to determining the child care-related problems that families of children with ASD face (which is done in the empirical portion of this monograph), it is also needed to review the child care policy context for children with disabilities in the United States.

This review starts by describing the various welfare state approaches modern countries have adopted, emphasizing their stability over time. The United States has adopted a liberal welfare state model that helps explain why some child care policies are quickly adopted while others are heavily modified before they are adopted, and why some are simply rejected. I review the history of such adoptions, modifications, and rejections for child care policies in the United States. Then I describe other elements of the American child care that may have salient implications for children with ASD, such as the implementation of the Americans with Disabilities Act. Finally, I use Hirschman's exit, voice, and loyalty framework (Hirschman 1970) to make sense of parental response or lack of response to child care policies. The chapter finishes with recommended policy strategies based on the empirical findings, the review of policies and parental response to the policies, and the four values articulated in the first paragraph of this chapter.

REVIEW OF CHILD CARE POLICIES

WELFARE STATE MODELS

Child care policies can be understood by contextualizing them within the larger framework of how governments act to ensure the welfare of private citizens. Because policy is an area known to be path-dependent, where decisions at one point in time change the trajectory of future developments (Pierson 2000), different countries practice different models of private welfare provision due to complex cultural and historical reasons. Although classifications of welfare state models have been criticized for favoring Nordic countries (Vincent and Ball 2006), there is broad consensus that in the West, there are three basic welfare state arrangements (Esping-Anderson 1999):

(1) The Nordic welfare state model is characterized by de-familiarization policies that make individuals independent from their families, policies that support gender equity, high

maternal employment with relatively strong glass ceiling effects, a strong safety net, and commitment to equality, financed with high levels of taxation. Sweden is the paradigmatic case. Typically, countries spend about one-third of their GDP financing this model (Howard 2003).

(2) The Southern European welfare state model is characterized by a familiarization strategy that promotes a household approach to individual welfare, encourages direct maternal care, and typically results in lower levels of female labor participation and higher unemployment, but better job security. Italy is characteristic of this approach. Typically, countries spend about one-quarter of their GDP financing this model (Howard 2003).

(3) The liberal welfare state model provides relatively small governmental assistance to those with demonstrated need, encourages participation in private markets, and forces those who are unemployed and need government support into work, while imposing relatively lower taxes. It results in high female labor participation with relatively weak glass ceiling effects. The model emphasizes growth over equality. The U.S. is the paradigmatic case. The United States spends around one-sixth of its GDP financing this model (Howard 2003).

Estimates of the size of the welfare state as a percentage of GDP have been criticized for failing to understand that Nordic models prefer direct assistance while the liberal welfare state approach favors indirect assistance to individuals. Indirect assistance takes various forms: (a) lower taxes on benefits received, as opposed to larger benefits and larger taxes, (b) tax expenditures (e.g. deductions or credits to promote socially desirable outcomes), as opposed to a more uniform tax treatment, (c) regulations that mandate private organizations to provide benefits (e.g. ADA), as opposed to directly funding the benefits through a government fund, and (d) giving private citizens the right to sue as a substitute for social insurance. Indeed, policy analysts have noted that litigation is an essential component of the American welfare state approach (Kagan and Axelrad 1997). Even with these indirect assistances factored into the calculation, the United States model accounts for a smaller portion of GDP than the Nordic model (Howard 2003).

The implementation of a welfare state model is highly path-dependent and resistant to change in part because it is founded on strongly held cultural values and in part because it is the result of the country's overall political and civic institutional arrangement. Some countries have had fairly pure models (e.g. Sweden) while other countries implement consciously designed mixed models (e.g. Germany), but all do so in a stable manner. Thus, it is rare to find countries that switch from one welfare state model to another, the exception being the United Kingdom before and after Margaret Thatcher. The United States has been a stable liberal welfare state.

Within each country, the consensus about its basic welfare state model ebbs and flows, with different administrations leaving their mark on child care policies. Those changes are the results of how issues are framed, the legacy of the existing institutional approach, norms and ideas about women's role in society, eugenic concerns about the societal desirability of children from specific subpopulations (e.g. immigrant and low-income), pro-natalist pressures, and the formation and power of various interest groups (White 2002; Naumann 2005; Ellingsater 2007; White 2009). In addition, the economic context is very important to why countries pass specific child care policies. For example, countries with higher levels of unemployment find ways to subsidize mothers staying at home longer, either through generous leave policies or through direct subsidies for stay-at-home parents. These policies are seen not only as family policy but also as labor policies to reduce the number of people in the labor force, and thus improve the unemployment rate (White 2009).

In general, child care policies have been categorized into two large groups (Lewis 2009): time-to-care policies that support the choice of parents to leave work to care for their children, and time-to-work polices that support the choice of parents to have other people care for their children so they can work. As mentioned before, the liberal welfare model supports time-to-work policies for anyone who needs governmental assistance, although it tolerates time-to-care policies for those who can afford them. Within time-to-work policies, we find a growing emphasis on child development in the last two decades.

THE CURRENT CHILD CARE POLICY FRAMEWORK

In the United States, there have been several attempts to include child care policies that would fit the Nordic state model better than the liberal welfare state. These policies are characterized by universal coverage, wide subsidies, and equality of access, relying often, although not always, on publicly provided services. During the political process these various attempts either have failed to become official policy or have been substantially scaled down to better fit the liberal state sensitivities of the American public. Overall, the process reflects that Americans are deeply conflicted about de-familiarization and support assistance mostly for those who are working, provided that taxes remain relatively low.

Indeed, public opinion polls report that the majority of Americans endorse that (a) the parents should be the primary influence on their children and (b) that mothers are the best caregivers for their infants and toddlers, while (c) supporting child care assistance for poor mothers who are expected to work rather than care for their children (Opinion Research Corporation International 1999; Sylvester 2001; Public Agenda 2000; Robison 2002). These results are very much in line with the liberal welfare state provision of services for those who need help, while emphasizing work over direct care whenever governmental assistance is needed.

One reason child researchers and advocates push for comprehensive entitlements in child care is that they are profoundly concerned about the impact of the liberal welfare state model on the poor. This concern is particularly salient in the context of limited intergenerational mobility. Despite the reality of the American dream for a few Americans, there is accumulating evidence that intergenerational mobility for society as a whole is hindered by the modern liberal welfare state.

Economists measure intergenerational mobility by estimating the intergenerational elasticity (IGE) in earnings between fathers and sons. The U.S. IGE has been estimated at 0.4—although some estimates are as high as 0.6—compared to levels of 0.2 for Nordic countries. The Nordic countries have lower IGEs precisely because their aggressive taxation and redistribution models prevent the accumulation and inheritance of economic opportunities to the same degree as countries with the more unregulated liberal welfare model. An IGE of 0.4 means that it would take three generations (about seventy-five years) for a family at 75% below the national income to reach the national average (it would take one hundred thirty-five years for an IGE of 0.6) (Solon 2002; Mazumder 2005). Thus, the liberal state model not only leads to wider inequalities of income but also to a larger stability of those inequalities over a longer period of time.

HISTORY OF COMPREHENSIVE ENTITLEMENTS ATTEMPTS

COMPREHENSIVE CHILD DEVELOPMENT ACT

In 1972, the U.S. Congress passed the Comprehensive Child Development Act (CCDA), which would have ostensibly provided universal access to child care. The CCDA never became law because it was vetoed by President Nixon. It is noteworthy that Nixon's communication on the occasion highlighted that the passage of the act would have weakened families and resulted in a communal, soviet-style approach to child rearing—a de-familiarization argument (Rosenberg 1992). Three years later, after Nixon's resignation, a scaled-down version of the CCDA legislation, the Child and Family Act of 1975, passed both houses but was vetoed by President Ford on similar grounds (Klein 1992). For many years, the failure to pass these bills was considered an important precedent that prevented any further attempts to provide comprehensive child care provision in the United States (Zigler, Marsland, and Lord 2009). This policy process is a textbook example of path dependency.

FAMILY MEDICAL LEAVE ACT

In 1993, the Family Medical Leave Act (FMLA) was originally proposed as a comprehensive, paid parental leave entitlement. Yet, it was passed in a substantially diminished form from its original concept by both exempting a sizable number of employers (e.g. small businesses) and providing no compensation for the leave. Thus, in the United States, family leave is largely a middle-class benefit for those who can afford to take it (very few people actually take it) (Waldvogel 1999; Han and Waldvogel 2003), as opposed to the general entitlement that paid parental leave is in many other countries. It is an example of how the liberal welfare state tolerates time-to-care policies for those who need no governmental assistance but does not encourage caring over work by offering direct assistance.

UNIVERSAL PRESCHOOL

A third, more current and complex, example of attempting to enact a comprehensive entitlement in child care is the multistate expansion of universal preschool. Although the original approach to universal preschool was to provide preschool for all, the current implementation of universal preschool is far from universal. It varies state by state, with many states opting for preschool for at-risk children or requiring that some percentage of funds be used to pay private providers (Barnett et al. 2009), compromises that fit the U.S. liberal state model's reliance on markets and governmental aid only for those with demonstrated need.

The case of universal preschool is more complex because of the way the United States funds and operates K-12 public education. Indeed, the success of universal preschool as a comprehensive entitlement has depended and will depend on whether preschool is framed as educational or child care policy. K-12 public education is a well-established anomaly to the liberal state model in the United States. Enacted in a period of American history when public schools were perceived as necessary to incorporate a massive influx of immigrant children into American culture and values, the K-12 system became stable through the Blaine Amendments to many state constitutions (DeForrest 2003; Buckley 2004), prohibiting the use of public funds in religious schools. Although the attempt to pass a Blaine Amendment at the federal level failed, subsequent interpretations of the First Amendment separated church and state in K-12 education in a far more rigid manner than is the case for virtually all other areas of U.S. policy. Thus, while no federal money is allowed to fund religious K-12 schools, federal financial aid follows students to religious colleges, and federal Medicare payments reimburse doctors at religiously affiliated hospitals. In sum, the public school system is a historical policy anomaly in a country that relies on private markets and targets assistance based on income status. Today, the entitlement is supported by a strong unionized constituency.

Regardless of the history, Americans accept direct government provision of K-12 public education in a universal, publicly provided manner. Thus, if universal preschool is perceived as adding a grade to K-12 within that already accepted system of K-12 education, it has a better likelihood of becoming a universal entitlement than if the policy is framed as child care policy. The relabeling of child care as early childhood education and the K-12 system as the preK-12 system is part of this wider strategy to foster wide acceptance of a large entitlement among the citizenry.

This approach is quite consistent with the notion that policy is path-dependent (Pierson 2000) and that new institutional infrastructure is built on previously enacted and widely accepted institutional structures. Researchers measure the degree of institutionalization on three metrics: prominence (wide acceptance by the public), horizontal linkages to other policies or programs, and vertical linkages with accepted norms (White 2002). On all three counts, American public schools are highly institutionalized and are thus institutional infrastructures that would be very hard to dismantle. Indeed, the approach of reframing child care as essential for child readiness and academic success has been tried repeatedly, from the claims of Head Start to Educare, a Colorado partnership that promotes quality of child care (Zigler, Marsland, and Lord 2009). Once preschool has been successfully introduced in the majority of states, advocates will likely advocate for its extension to full-day preschool. To the extent that the implementation of kindergarten is a relevant historical precedent (Montes 1996; Ross 1976), it will take more than six decades before a full implementation of universal, full-day preschool occurs in the United States.

21ST CENTURY SCHOOLS

The latest attempt to provide a national system of care was Zigler's School of the 21st Century. Zigler's view on the American decentralized system of care is both well-known and highly influential: "Our child care system—or nonsystem is a better description—is an incoherent, heterogeneous collection of hundreds of thousands of settings and services" (Zigler 1990). However influential, this view portrayed a societal norm as an aberration, because Americans rely on such an incoherent, heterogeneous collection of providers for the provision of the vast majority of goods and services, including medicine and higher education. The School of the 21st Century model was Zigler's approach to "simplify and organize child care" (Zigler 1990). In his own words, "The best way I know to do this is to make the core of the system a known and trusted institution, namely, the American school" (Zigler 1990). It is no coincidence that both the preschool movement and the School of the 21st Century have similar strategies to foster wide acceptance of a large entitlement.

The School of the 21st Century model was proposed as a second system in public schools that would operate after hours and would have a different administration. Although after-school comprehensive, school-based care has been in operation in Sweden for decades, the parallels with the Nordic welfare state models were not heavily emphasized. The model School of the 21st Century would offer home visitation, create a network of private family child care providers under the supervision of the public school, contract out services to Head Start and similar providers for group care, and provide appropriate resource and referrals. In economic terms, the model amounted to the centralization of the child care industry under governmental control. Such a model did not fit the liberal welfare state that relies on private markets. Thus, what Congress actually enacted was quite different.

The 21st Century Community Learning Centers (21CCLC) is the only federal program that funds after-school services. It was passed in 1998 as a community program that shared the resources of public schools (e.g. labs, gymnasiums, etc.) with the community at large, but later its focus was narrowed by its inclusion into the No Child Left Behind (NCLB) legislation to concentrate the after-school services on high-needs students and target measurable increases on participants' standardized test scores. The program allows for additional services to the core academic program (e.g. tutoring), including sports, arts, music, drug prevention, and the like. This history is an example of regulatory capture by the K-12 system and adaptation to the K-12 accountability goals while serving high-needs communities, which is consistent with the liberal welfare state model. Indeed, the history of regulatory capture is quite similar to the rather drastic adaptation of kindergarten from a private community program that offered home visitation to just another grade in the American public schools at the beginning of the 20th century (Montes 1996).

The 21CCLC is a $1.1 billion program funded by No Child Left Behind. States receive the money based on their Title I appropriations. The State Education departments have wide discretion on how to use the funds and how much to spend. Two-thirds of the grantees are public school systems capturing these additional funds to essentially offer tutoring programs. Per-pupil cost is relatively low, less than $1,500. Regular attendance is an issue, with only 55% of the students in the centers attending regularly (Afterschool Alliance 2009). Consistent with the liberal welfare state model within the comprehensive entitlement of K-12, most of the recipients attend high-poverty, low-performing schools, and the focus of the program is academic remediation and enrichment for this academically at-risk population. A national, matched-design 2003 U.S. Department of Education study found "negligible effects on academic or behavioral outcomes of the students" (US Department of Education 2003). In 2004, a continuation of the same study found few effects on academic achievement and "mixed effects on negative behavior for students," meaning that "some estimates pointed to higher levels of negative behaviors for middle school students, while others indicated no differences between treatment and comparison groups" (Dynarski et al. 2004). In the medical field, such findings would warrant serious investigation for characteristics of patients for whom the program is contraindicated. I was unable to find any other comprehensive national studies since 2004.

In sum, it is fair to say that although prominent academics and advocates have proposed a number of Nordic-style entitlements for child care, each time the legislative process has substantially modified them to fit better with either the liberal welfare state model or the American public school system, or both. Other U.S. child care policies fit the liberal welfare state model better than these comprehensive approaches either because they target children who have been defined as needy in some way, or because they rely on private markets and individual choice, or both.

HEAD START AND EARLY HEAD START

Head Start is by far the most controversial program in American child care policy. The program was a product of the War on Poverty, and its main original goal was to change IQ scores of impoverished children. There is controversy even on the origins of the program, with some suggesting that a community action program was "diverted from its true purpose as a community action program by craven liberal politicians, elitist academic developmental psychologists, and an American political system that would not tolerate true reform" (Harmon 2004; Kuntz 1998; Greenberg 1990). Over the years, Head Start has been researched more than any other program, and it would be fair to say that results have been mixed, above all in the core areas of intelligence and future academic school performance (Currie and Thomas 1995; Ellsworth Associates Inc. 1994; Zigler and Muenchow 1994). In particular, there has been much ink spent in discussing the fade-out of Head Start effects over time (Lee et al. 1990; Lee and Loeb 1995). In response to this checkered pattern of results, there has been a widening of the program goals, increasing regulation and measurement, and funding for larger, better studies that could settle the question of whether the program works. There is no doubt, however, that as the program's goals have widened to a variety of familial and health outcomes, the program has become substantially more expensive to the American taxpayer.

Since 1966, the first year of full-year implementation, Head Start has expanded from serving three-quarters of a million children in 1966 to almost a million children in 2009. In that same period, the inflation-adjusted per-pupil cost has quadrupled to the officially reported 2009 cost of $7,600 (Office of Head Start - Administration for Children and Families 2010).

The latest federally funded study on Head Start was recently concluded. This comprehensive, nationally representative study randomized five thousand Head Start-eligible children (three- and four-year-olds) into Head Start or a control group. Control group children enrolled in whatever programs their families chose, including in Head Start after one year. Researchers measured the children's and parents' performance on more than three hundred academic, socio-emotional, health, and parenting outcomes during the Head Start years and in kindergarten and first grade. There were positive results during the Head Start year, but no systematic evidence of efficacy in kindergarten or first grade, and two negative impacts were reported (US Department of Health and Human Services. Administration of Children and Families 2010). Subgroup information found that the program had the worst outcomes for three-year-old children whose parents reported moderate depressive symptoms: "These children experienced negative impacts across the cognitive, socio-emotional, and health domains" (US Department of Health and Human Services, Administration of Children and Families 2010). Head Start appears to be contraindicated for this subpopulation. Hopefully, steps will be taken to ensure children likely to be harmed by the program are not eligible to receive it.

In addition, a newer threat to the continuing funding for Head Start is the emergence of universal preschools, which are cheaper on a per-pupil expenditure basis and appear to have comparable results (Henry, Gordon, and Rickman 2006). As universal preschool expands, questions naturally arise about the relevance of Head Start programs. Thus, it is not coincidence that the push for universal preschool coincides with the push for Early Head Start (Head Start for infants and toddlers).

In 2002, Timothy Hacsi reviewed the history of Head Start in a much-cited book, *Children as Pawns*. After finding the evidence of program efficacy inconclusive, Hacsi argued for quality improvements:

> Whether or not Head Start is making a significant difference for its children now, it probably will make a difference if we focus on improving its quality. Until we find better ways of helping poor children do well in school, this seems a reasonable thing to do. If we are truly concerned with educating disadvantaged children, one significant step would be to make sure there are places for all in high-quality preschool programs (Hacsi 2002).

In 2011, I do not believe much progress has been made. Alternative uses of the Head Start per-pupil expenditure are not considered; the policy options debated are either defunding Head Start or ongoing improvement of the quality, a theme as old as Head Start itself. This is unfortunate, because $7,600 constitutes 52% of the annual income for a single mother with a Head Start-eligible child. Such a large proportion of the family budget may have alternative uses that increase the family's welfare more than attending Head Start. For example, placed in a privately held 529 account during the preschool years, $7000 would grow to be a sizeable down payment for college fourteen years later. Thus, alternative ways to assist the Head Start eligible population must be considered and not just additional modifications to the program which in the past have resulted in increased cost but no additional lasting benefits. I reach this conclusion reluctantly, because as one of my reviewers pointed out, Head Start provides services for many children with ASD who have few other places to go.

The results of a recent report from the Government Accountability Office (GAO) on fraud do not help. The GAO conducted thirteen eligibility tests by creating fictitious families that did not meet Head Start eligibility criteria and who attempted to enroll into the program. In sixty-one percent of the cases (eight out of thirteen), families were enrolled because Head Start staff instructed the families to misrepresent their incomes. In four of the cases, the "GAO later received doctored documents that excluded income information originally provided to the Head Start staff" (Kutz 2010).

In sum, had these results followed a five thousand-person randomized trial on a $7 billion publicly funded medical treatment provided by the pharmaceutical industry, surely we would have seen such treatments withdrawn from the market. Whether it is the fidelity of the Head Start implementation, the design of the program, the training of the staff, or the schools that Head Start children attend after their participation in the program, Head Start does not appear to be a long-term solution for intergenerational mobility in the United States. It is a symptom of the ongoing Head Start malaise that these results only prompt further research and discussion. At a minimum, adverse event reporting ought to be systematically implemented throughout Head Start to determine if the program is contraindicated for any other subpopulations.

Fortunately, the results for Early Head Start are more positive, though more preliminary. Early Head Start serves fewer than one hundred thousand children at a cost similar to that of Head Start. It is a two-generation program. A 2002 randomized trial found moderate positive effects of the program during the Early Head Start experience in a variety of domains ranging from parenting to cognitive development. Whether these results last is unknown. The program seemed to be particularly effective for African-Americans, mothers and children who entered the program while the mother was pregnant, and children with a moderate number of demographic risk factors. This information could be used to target the program more precisely to those most likely to benefit.

Accepting that contraindications may exist, and targeting the program to the best candidates for treatment is probably the best way to enhance the effectiveness of any program. Although no one has a right to receive an intervention that does not work, well understood solidarity with children in poverty means an ongoing commitment to develop new interventions for those subpopulations that cannot benefit from existing programs, rather than offer to them an ineffective program.

THE CHILD CARE AND DEVELOPMENT FUND

The Child Care and Development Fund (CCDF) is a $5 billion integrated entitlement created by the Personal Responsibility and Work Opportunity Reconciliation Act of 1996. It encompasses the Child Care and Development Block Grant Act of 1990. The CCDF also received an additional $2 billion from the American Recovery and Reinvestment Act of 2009. At the federal level, CCDF is administered by the Child Care Bureau, but, consistent with the Block Grant concept, states have great latitude to implement the act. CCDF provides subsidies for all types of legal child care providers—including unlicensed care—that meet basic health and safety requirements. The program has a wider reach than Head Start, serving around 1.7 million children annually (Child Care Bureau 2010; Office of Child Care 2008).

Typically, states spend around 10% on quality improvements, primarily via the development and implementation of quality rating and improvement systems (QRIS) that are sometimes used to provide financial incentives via tiered reimbursement programs. Eligible families must be low-income, as defined by the state, but below 85% of the median state income, have children in the birth to thirteen-year-old range, and be working or in training or education.

There has been extensive research on many aspects of the subsidy program. Research has found that recipients of subsidies tend to have children younger than age six, who are receiving or have received Temporary Assistance for Needy Families (TANF) support in the past, are single-parent households, are African-American households, or use center-based care child care arrangements (Shlay et al. 2002, 2004; U.S. General Accounting Office 2003; Lawrence and Lee Kreader 2005; Schaefer, Lee Kreader, and Collins 2005). Interestingly, not all constraints are based on demographics or income; there is evidence that "parents with higher tolerance for the hassles that families may encounter in applying for and maintaining child care subsidies appear more likely to use subsidies" (Lawrence and Lee Kreader 2005). A GAO undercover investigation, similar to the one conducted on Head Start, discovered that the CCDF's implementation in five states was vulnerable to fraud in the use of unlicensed providers (GAO 2010). Yet, the program is popular with parents, and communities often run out of subsidies.

The CCDF model matches the liberal welfare state model in its reliance on private markets and its assistance for beneficiaries with demonstrated need who are willing to work.

CHILD CARE AND DEPENDENT TAX CREDITS AND CHILD CARE TAX CREDITS

Consistent with the liberal state framework, indirect child care assistance is provided via tax expenditures at the federal level, and also in some states at the state level.

Tax relief for care expenses started during the post-World War II era. During the Clinton administration, in the context of welfare reform, the child and dependent tax credit was refocused on assisting parents who work. Thus, the credit can only be used to reimburse parents who identify an external care provider—it cannot be either parent or an adult dependent of the parents (e.g. a nineteen-year-old child). One-earner couples are not eligible. The credit also penalizes larger families since it can provide up to 35% of qualifying expenses, until $3,000 for one qualifying child and $6,000 for two or more (in 2009) (IRS 2010, 2010). Parents with additional children do not receive any additional assistance. The credit phases down to 20% as income increases and can never be more than the income of the lesser-earning spouse. Most importantly, the credit is not refundable. Thus, the lowest income households that owe no taxes do not benefit from it. It is a $2 to $3 billion expenditure, and about four million households claim it (McKenna 2010). The credit is broader than child care and also covers dependent care (e.g. elder care). Perhaps because of the requirement to identify the care provider, many eligible families do not claim it.

At the time the child care and dependent tax credit was reformed, the strategy was criticized for discriminating against parents who wished to stay at home. Assistance for stay-at-home parents, although directly subsidized in other welfare state models (e.g. Germany, France), does not fit well in the liberal state framework, in that it discourages parental employment and reliance on private child care markets, nor does it fit the economic context because the United States has a relatively low unemployment rate by international standards, even when it rises to 10%.

During the George W. Bush administration, parents were given a substantially increased and refundable child tax credit. A reform of the child tax credit enacted in 1998, the 2001 version indexed refundability to inflation (Esenwein 2010). While not specifically designed as a child care tax expenditure, it provides funds that may be used to finance any child care decision, including the decision to stay home with the child. Because it is refundable, it provides assistance even to parents without tax liability. The credit also does not discriminate against families with more than two children, allowing a per-child credit. The credit is currently at $1000 per child, with a phase out for married couples at $110,000 and $75,000 for individual taxpayers.

Of special interest to parents of children with ASD are developments in various states to provide a special needs child tax credit that can be utilized to provide additional assistance for parents of children with special needs. Previous research has shown that (a) parents of children with ASD spend substantially more on their children than other parents in a variety of educational and medical interventions (Liptak, Stuart, and Auinger 2006) and that (b) having a child with ASD is associated with a loss of household income (Montes and Halterman 2008). Therefore, a federal tax credit for parents of children with special needs would certainly assist in leveling the playing field.

UNFUNDED MANDATES: THE AMERICANS WITH DISABILITIES ACT

The Americans with Disabilities Act (ADA) provides extensive coverage for individuals with disabilities, prohibiting discrimination based on disability in employment, public accommodations, commercial facilities, transportation, telecommunications, and state and local government. Child care centers and providers are covered under Title III. The ADA prohibits exclusion, segregation, and unequal treatment in child care settings on the basis of a disability. ADA does not specify disabilities by name; rather, the attorney for the child must show that the disability impairs one or more life activities, including learning, socialization, speaking, working, and performing manual tasks. Given the diagnostic criteria for ASD, children with ASD should have no trouble meeting this definition.

The ADA was amended in 2008 primarily because a number of court decisions had narrowed the definition of disability. The amendments were intended to restore the original intent of the legislation (ADA AA 2008).

Child care centers can refuse accommodations for two reasons: by claiming the child with disabilities presents a direct threat to peers or program staff, or by claiming that accommodations would substantially alter their program (Shipley 2001). Importantly, all child care providers need to do an individualized assessment and not simply assume that because the child has a particular disability or the provider has been unable to accommodate other children with the same disability, they cannot accommodate this particular child (US Department of Justice). Under ADA, parents can sue child care providers and/or they can file a complaint with the U.S. Department of Justice, who sometimes refers cases to mediation (Shipley 2001).

ADA has been used successfully to open child care centers for children with HIV and children with allergies (Shipley 2001). There have been relatively few attempts to use it to open child care centers to children with ASD. A notable exception is the *Jordan Burriola v. Greater Toledo YMCA* case.

In *Burriola*, a single working mother sued the YMCA after the YMCA expelled her eight-year-old child with high-functioning autism, Jordan. The YMCA had refused free ASD training and basic accommodations for Jordan such as providing a schedule of activities ahead of time. The YMCA defended itself using both the direct threat and the modification-of-program legal defenses. In this case, the judge granted a preliminary injunction that forced the YMCA to readmit Jordan and to train its staff. The judge dismissed the direct threat defense not because Jordan was not misbehaving but because, had reasonable accommodation been provided, Jordan probably would have behaved well. Importantly, the judge made this determination based on ASD expert testimony from the teachers at his school. The judge dismissed the substantial alteration defense on the grounds that the YMCA already provided needed one-on-one time with any child at the program at some time and thus such personalized attention to Jordan would not constitute undue burden or fundamentally alter the program. In reading the decision, one is often shocked by sheer unwillingness to accommodate the child in defiance of ADA (Zraik 2011). Certainly, I do not believe that this particular YMCA would have acted in this way if the child had a visible disability.

Although there have been no studies to determine how common Jordan's plight is, evidence from expulsions in early childhood for behavior problems suggests that the providers' preference for expulsion over providing reasonable accommodations may be quite widespread (Gilliam and Shahar 2006). In a survey of child care providers, Helen Ward reported that providers wanted to accommodate children with behavior problems but blamed lack of resources and training as reasons not to do so (Ward et al. 2006). Although child care providers have the right to expel any child who is a direct threat (Shipley 2001), it requires careful discernment to understand when the threat is caused by the providers' refusal to comply with ADA in the first place. I think it is fair to state that, in regards to child care, the promise of ADA has not been realized for children with ASD.

OTHER ELEMENTS OF THE AMERICAN CHILD CARE SYSTEM

There are other federal child care programs that are either targeted to specific subpopulations such as children of military families or other federal employees, or provide funds for specific services such as subsidized meals in child care centers. Similarly, the federal government allows, and many employers offer, the opportunity to save for child care expenses in pretax saving plans (McKenna 2010).

Non-statutory elements of the American child care system are often neglected by policy analysts because they consist of actions by private parties that are not required by American law. Yet, some of these actions are essential for the viability of the decentralized American child care system, and indeed they are the object of public policy in other countries (e.g. France). Chief among them is the role of job flexibility. Businesses provide job flexibility in a variety of circumstances and for a variety of jobs. While flexibility is mostly available to educated workers, its presence allows parents to coordinate care in ways that are not possible for those who work in inflexible jobs.

Equally important, particularly in the American jurisprudence system where legal precedents and class action lawsuits can dramatically extend the coverage of laws, is the role of parental litigation on behalf of children with ASD. Anyone who has observed how the rights of parents of children with special needs under IDEA have expanded thanks to litigation should have no doubts about the potential for child care under applicable laws such as ADA or section 504 of the Rehabilitation Act. Litigation, within the American context, initially confers de facto advantages mostly to middle and upper class parents who can afford to litigate, but its benefits often trickle down through prevention of litigation by corporations and organizations, particularly when the credible threat of lawsuits exist, as well as by legal precedent and expansive clarifications or interpretations of the applicability of existing law to children with ASD attending privately or publicly provided child care.

Finally, it is important to realize that our knowledge of the costs and investments that parents make in child care is severely limited due to the "historic invisibility of caregiving work" (Meyers and Durfee 2006). In particular, parental caregiving time, as any other unremunerated household production activity, is explicitly excluded from the GDP or any other standard measure of economic activity. Thus, non-remunerated caregiving labor by parents, relatives, or friends is often taken for granted or minimized in policy discussions. Yet, the fact that it is uncounted does not mean that it is unimportant. Were these invisible contributions to become absent overnight, there is little doubt that there would ensue a true child care crisis in America. Thus, these inputs are essential for the viability of the current American child care system, and specific public policy proposals should be evaluated for their impact on this important but unmeasured part of the American economy.

THE PARENTAL RESPONSE TO POLICY: VOICE, EXIT, AND LOYALTY

Any analysis of a policy framework is incomplete without a review of how the intended beneficiaries react to the policies. Beneficiaries are not inert, and their reactions may in some cases have unintended iatrogenic consequences. In this section, I propose Hirschman's exit, voice, and loyalty framework as a theoretical lens to understand parental response to child care policy.

Hirschman's framework has been used in a variety of policy contexts (Furaker 2009; Okamoto and Wilkes 2008; Langston 2002), including education (Wilson 2009). In 1970, Hirschman analyzed the relationship between democratic processes of demand (voice) and choice-based processes (exit) (Hirschman 1970). In particular, Hirschman was concerned that choice mechanisms may lead to a diminished voice either because citizens who exit do not learn how to participate in the political process, or because the best prepared citizens choose to exit, leaving behind citizens with fewer resources to advocate.

Although in well-functioning organizations, loyalty to the organization will result in appropriate voice and reform, in dysfunctional cases loyalty can lead to both diminished voice—not wanting to criticize—and diminished exit. Because the parental response to child care policy is characterized by both neglect of some policy options and overuse of others, resulting in waiting lists, Hirschman's framework appeared particularly suitable as a theoretical lens.

Later theorists (Dowding et al. 2000) have complemented the original framework by incorporating a dynamic and path-dependent aspect to the choice of voice versus exit. Thus, if voice is ineffective, people are more likely to choose exit subsequently; and conversely, if exit is either unsuccessful or unsatisfactory, they are more likely to pursue voice.

A HIRSCHMANNIAN ANALYSIS

Perhaps the most important phenomena that a Hirschmannian analysis of parental response to child care policies must accomplish is to explain why there is no parental movement (no voice, in Hirschman's typology) for comprehensive child care reform in spite of the media consistently identifying a recurrent, unsolved child care crisis (McClure 2011; Murphy and Lacy 2009; Goldrick-Rab 2010). Although there are some organizations that lobby for child care reform (e.g. MomsRising, Mothers Movement Online), they are often viewed as partisan (Zigler, Marsland, and Lord 2009) and are not specifically focused on child care issues; rather, their main focus is to end workplace discrimination against mothers (MomsRising 2011). Where is the bipartisan, grassroots parental movement to solve the child care crisis? Why is there diminished voice among parents?

PARENTAL RESPONSE TO POLICY

In my analysis, there are three reasons for low parental involvement: (a) age segmentation, (b) the lack of political diversity in academia, and (c) the differences in the notion of quality between parents and experts.

First, by framing the child care policies as an age-based series of decisions (e.g. child care for infants, preschool for three- and four-year-olds, school for older children) parents have little personal incentive to invest in having their voices heard. Any foreseeable result of their actions will have few personal benefits for their own children, who will have aged out when any policy changes are finally made. Intentionally or unintentionally, segmenting child care decisions by age promotes parental opting-out behavior (exit) while leaving the political involvement (voice) in child care policies to those organizations that advocate for or serve children of the same age year after year. Increasing professionalization of providers aligns their views with those of professors who grant them professional status.

Second, some child care proposals, such as the School of the 21st Century, do not represent the full political spectrum of the American public. Many research studies have shown that politically conservative voices are seriously underrepresented in academia, particularly in the social sciences and humanities, and particularly those who self-identify as classical liberals (Klein and Stern 2008; Zipp and Fenwick 2006; Klein and Stern 2005, 2005; Hamilton and hargens 1993; Gross and Simmons 2007). A classical liberal is a person who supports limited government and freedom of religion, press, and assembly, free markets (Hudelson 1998), the philosophical underpinnings of the U.S. welfare state's reliance on markets, and assistance only to the needy. In contrast, the sparse research on public opinion toward government spending on child care indicates that a person's political ideology and party identification are among the strongest drivers of political support for expansion of child care expenditures (Henderson et al. 1995). These individual-level political value variables are rarely collected in empirical studies. Their information is often proxied by race and economic status variables. Race and income are more predictive of state child care policy than state wealth, governor's political affiliation, or number of women representatives in legislatures (Ng 2006). Thus, how child care spending is framed with respect to larger political values is essential to explain public support for the proposals (Jacoby 2000). The lack of political diversity in academia often results in frames that are largely unpersuasive to large sectors of the American public.

Parents, represented in all political parties and ideologies, are unlikely to uniformly support child care proposals that the average American citizen views as too centralized or too expensive within the context of the U.S. economy.

Third, differences in the view of quality between parents and researchers/policymakers may lead parents to have low involvement. Emlen has criticized the field of child care for its reliance on two measures of quality that exclude parental considerations of quality: the Early Childhood Environment Rating Scale (ECERS) and the Infant/Toddler Environment Rating Scale (ITERS) (Emlen 2010). Despite much rhetoric that quality implies better development for children, the actual correlations between ECERS and child outcomes are very modest (Burchinal et al. 2009). Modest correlations imply that many children in low-quality environments, as measured by ECERS, gain as much as children in high-quality environments and vice versa. In a textbook example of Kuhn's theory that, when faced with disconfirming evidence, scientists often modify their theories minimally to accommodate the troubling facts to scientific orthodoxy, child care researchers have greater hopes for stronger correlations between child outcomes and a newer measure, the Classroom Assessment Scoring System (CLASS). Recent research, however, suggests that there may be unmeasured quality domains not captured by either the CLASS or the ECERS (Chien et al. 2010). Whether this is evidence of disconfirmation to a much cherished scientific theory (*ceteris paribus*, higher quality implies higher outcomes) or whether, as researchers claim, it will be explained by unmeasured quality variables, I do not know. What I can observe, however, is that the pattern of endless measurement refinement in the face of disconfirming scientific evidence is quite consistent with the prior stage before a scientific revolution in Kuhn's well-accepted typology of how science develops (Kuhn 1962). Based on the modest correlations between quality and outcomes measures, there seems to be much evidence that many children gain in what researchers define as low-quality environments. The scientific community is unwilling to abandon a theory on which a large amount of public policy expansion (e.g. the universal preschool movement) is predicated, and thus posit unmeasured quality domains that would explain the inconsistency in the data. Unless such quality domains are found quickly and result in robust correlations, the accumulation of data will persuade younger scientists that higher quality (ECERS, CLASS, or any other similar measure) does not imply higher outcomes for children. If Kuhn is right, at some point the accumulations of data will trump theory, and we will see a major shift in theories relating professional standards of quality and child outcomes. Such a shift would surely impact public policy.

These developments in the scientific community are germane to the current discussion because for several decades researchers, professional organizations, and the media defined quality as whatever researchers can measure and then reported that (a) parents' assessments of quality correlate weakly with ECERS ratings done by trained observers, even when the parental questionnaire is explicitly constructed based on the ECERS and parents rate each item in the ECERS as uniformly important (Cryer, Tietze, and Wessels 2002), (b) parents systematically overestimate quality (Cryer, Tietze, and Wessels 2002; Browne Miller 1990; Cryer and Burchinal 1997), and (c) the quality of child care in America is mediocre. These statements hinge on valid measures of quality that are highly correlated with future child outcomes. Those measures do not yet exist. Consequently, a more accurate statement would be that American child care is mediocre on quality measures modestly correlated with child outcomes. The hidden theme that is central to our discussion resides in the way such statements are typically worded. When differences between researchers and parents are found, the differences are tacitly described as parental errors from true quality (e.g. "parents overestimate quality"), where true quality is tacitly assumed to coincide with researchers' measurement.

By far, the best counterargument to these observations, provided by a reviewer, is that the ECERS measures quality domains that are important *regardless of child outcomes*, and that no child should attend low ECERS environments because we have decided such environments do not meet basic community norms. Such an argument has the virtue of being consistent with known facts, support current policy, and make a great deal of common sense.

In any case, given that that parents, children, child care staff members, and researchers define quality differently (Ceglowski and Bacigalupa 2002), it is unclear whose version of quality the liberal welfare state should endorse and why, particularly when correlations between researcher-quality and outcomes are so modest. Nevertheless, because historically researchers' views of quality have dominated much public discourse on child care, we can understand why parents are unlikely to engage in an issue where their own notions of quality are dismissed out of hand as uninformed.

There is one exception regarding the use of voice as a strategy by parents. This is the case of parents of children with special needs. Children with special needs often need very expensive services that may last a lifetime. Because of this foreseeable, recurrent, high cost, parents of children with special needs cannot effectively exit and can potentially reap greater benefits from direct involvement in policymaking (voice) than parents can of normally developing children. In short, parents of children with special needs often really need assistance beyond what their household incomes can provide, and this is true even among upper middle class families who have enough resources to organize.

Even in these cases, we see parental involvement in the form of advocacy and lawsuits primarily against the public school system and, typically, not against child care organizations. This behavior, voice about school policy but not child care, is also the result of public policy and not some idiosyncratic behavior of the parents. In this case, the Individuals with Disabilities Education Act (IDEA) regulates the provision of services to children ages three to twenty-one through the public schools. This policy structure has three clear effects. First, it makes the public school the hub of services and makes all concerns about disability to be artificially focused on academic performance or classroom behavior. The key document is the Individualized Education Plan (IEP), which must list services the child will receive and be reasonably calculated to provide student *educational* benefit (Etscheidt 2003). Second, the legislation de facto excludes most community settings as avenues to receive funding or provide services for children with disabilities because the public schools are both the adjudicators and main providers of services. Typically, schools decide to use the funds to support their own existing services. Those decisions surprise no one, because there is an inescapable conflict of interest implicit in IDEA that makes schools beneficiaries of their own adjudication decisions. Third, by making the school the adjudicator of governmental assistance, IDEA makes the school the focus of litigation. In this context, parents of children with ASD have been reported to account for a disproportionate number of the lawsuits against public schools. Not surprisingly, these lawsuits often attempt to extend services to the summer, beyond school hours, and beyond the school building. Consequently, IDEA results in the underfunding and underutilization of community systems, including child care services, and leaves parents to struggle to provide care and services for a child whose disability impairs functioning outside of the school year and before or after school hours.

Finally, there is a clear example of loyalty, in the Hirschmannian sense, in American child care policy. The very survival of Head Start is inexplicable without understanding that Head Start has a strong constituency that views the program as an essential entitlement earned during the hard-fought battle of the civil rights movement. In the Hirschmannian context, loyalty can lead to voice and reform, and there is no doubt Head Start has been reformed many times by those most loyal to it (Zigler and Valentine 1979; Zigler and Muenchow 1994; Zigler and Styfco 2004; Harmon 2004). Loyalty, however, may lead to diminished voice and diminished exit and can thus result in stagnation.

To a lesser degree, all federal programs and the preschool movement generate intense loyalty among a group of passionate advocates. Unfortunately, sometimes such passion leads to making unsustainable claims about the likely long-term societal effects of a particular program. For example, Head Start went through an over-promise phase when there was wide optimism about the ability of the program to solve societal ills. When the program could not deliver, it came under vigorous attacks (Hood 1992).

Currently, universal preschool is promised to substantially reduce incarceration rates, lower teenage pregnancy, and reduce the drop-out rate. As the Connecticut Governor stated, "It [preschool] will save millions of dollars on prisons we will not have to build" (Rell 2007). These claims are not unsupported; they are based on randomized studies and long-term follow-up studies (Barnett 1992). Unfortunately, the claim that early childhood education diminishes criminal behavior was also made by passionate advocates of universal kindergarten at the beginning of the 20th century. Reverend Newton, a tireless advocate, expressed it in remarkably modern language: "What the state spends in kindergarten, it will save in prisons" (Ross 1976). History has not been kind to this particular claim. The widespread dissemination of kindergarten coincided with some of the largest incarceration levels in U.S. history. The rise in incarceration levels were directly related to law enforcement policies, such as the three-strike laws. Whatever the positive impact of kindergarten, no one can argue that it has been a solution to the crime problem. The parallels with preschool show the dangers of making such long-term promises on the effects of early education programs on the future of society. Making claims that will lead the general public to view preschool as a panacea for societal ills will probably lead to discontent later on, as it did with Head Start. Thus, loyalty can be a double-edged sword.

SUGGESTED POLICY STRATEGIES

Parents of children with ASD struggle to provide child care for their children within the decentralized context that characterizes the U.S. system of child care. First, IDEA is absorbing most of the voice of parents of children with ASD in part because of attempts to expand its coverage to community settings. This phenomenon appears to be completely driven by existing policy and the conflict of interest schools face when they must adjudicate services for children with ASD. Thus, one of the suggested strategies is to look deeper at the IDEA legislation and find ways to resolve this conflict of interest. Not only would this result in better services in the community, but it would also likely reduce the litigation against public schools.

Second, clearly ADA is not implemented in child care settings. Because the liberal welfare state favors litigation over social insurance, if parents do not demand their children's rights under ADA with at least some credible threat of litigation, it is unlikely that much will change. To be fair, research has shown that many providers of care want to assist children with special needs but report they lack resources to do so (Ward et al. 2006). Thus, providers' *actual* willingness to pay for quality training is low. Weak effective demand results in a scarce supply of trainings offered at relatively high prices for high end providers.

Thus, one of my suggested strategies will ask for both a full implementation of ADA and assistance to accomplish it. I am aware that many in the disability rights community believe ADA has fallen short of its promise in many respects. Some groups are considering a return toward direct welfare provision as a main political strategy to improve the conditions of people with disabilities (Bagenstos 2004). I find the argument that direct welfare provision should be emphasized over adequate enforcement of ADA untenable in the current economic circumstances. This is one of the reasons why direct provision of services is not recommended as a viable strategy in this monograph, at least for the next few years, while enforcement of ADA is recommended in part, because it may be politically attractive to a bipartisan constituency precisely because much of the strategy depends on the behavior of nongovernmental actors.

While ADA will probably never be implemented fully with children with ASD, just as it falls short in many other areas, it seems to me that, as a nation, we could implement ADA far more than we are in child care settings on behalf of children with ASD. Doing so would facilitate access for children with ASD to the child care system and alleviate the burden of ASD on the family.

In particular, I suggest consideration of the following strategies to implement ADA in child care settings and to provide enough **assistance to providers to meet ADA requirements.**

a. **Consider policies that strengthen the civic and nonprofit sectors**, including the religious nonprofit sector, to assist families in meeting their child care needs, particularly for the low-income population and children with special needs. Children with ASD attend all these sectors and all will need assistance to meet ADA requirements.

b. **Within the context of the Child Care Development Fund, consider increased reimbursement for child care providers that are committed to inclusion and are currently serving a child with ASD whose family also meets income eligibility.** Low-income families of children with ASD are very unlikely to establish stable employment unless they can secure stable child care that meets their child's needs. Using some portion of the CCDF funds to incentivize the growth of trained child care providers for children with ASD may effectively assist families of children with ASD to secure better employment.

c. **Make high-quality, cost-effective training available to providers when and where they need it.** There is a need to develop high-quality, cost-effective training that meets the needs of providers. Many child care providers are women and minority owned businesses with small profit margins; thus, there is a need to provide the training at a price they can afford. The training needs to be brief and be available when and where it is needed. Because the 1% of children with ASD are geographically distributed throughout the country, the training must use new technologies (e.g. online) so that geographically distant child care providers can access it when they need it. It would be advantageous if professional organizations take a lead role in developing peer support and mentoring approaches in communities to help fellow providers become trained and appropriately use the training.

d. **Consider a national hotline to provide individualized mentoring and resources for providers needing assistance with ADA compliance, particularly in the areas of managing child behavior and developing executive functioning**. With current technology capabilities, such a hotline may be a web-based resource that offers not only information and materials but also direct distance mentoring on how to handle specific situations.

Second, to fully implement ADA, parents must have **affordable avenues to pursue the enforcement of their children's rights.**

a. **Form legal defense organizations** that are able to provide legal representation to parents of children with ASD at relatively low cost. No one is promoting litigation for its own sake. Unfortunately, sometimes litigation or the credible threat of litigation is needed to get compliance with ADA.

b. **Encourage parents of children with ASD to report violations of ADA to the U.S. Department of Justice. Autism organizations can provide essential information to parents of what their rights are under ADA and how to report violations.** It is essential that the U.S. government become aware of how large a problem exists, both to evaluate needs for training at the national level and because the current unmet needs are invisible to most of the political community.

c. **Facilitate changes in social norms regarding ADA and autism among child care providers.** Initially, this can be done by clarifying the obligations of child care providers under ADA with respect to children with special needs or behavioral problems, including ASD, or both, through the CCDF and the U.S. Department of Justice. Eventually, parent's groups and the general media can convey the message that expulsion is not an acceptable solution for children with ASD.

Third, comprehensive child care entitlements are unlikely to pass, particularly for a population of 1% of children. Thus, provision of financial assistance is most likely to occur within the context of a tax credit.

a. Legislatively, **consider a federal special needs child tax credit** to acknowledge that families of children with ASD or other disabilities have more expenditures and higher loss of income than comparable families.

LIST OF ABBREVIATIONS

ADA – Americans with Disabilities Act

AS – Asperger Syndrome

ASD – Autism Spectrum Disorder

IACC – Interagency Autism Coordinating Committee

IDEA – Individuals with Disabilities Education Act

IEP – Individualized Education Plan

PDD – Pervasive Developmental Disorder

PDD-NOS – Pervasive Developmental Disorder – Not Otherwise Specified

REFERENCES

ADA AA. *The ADA Amendment Act of 2008, Public Law 110-325* 2008. Available from www.access-board.gov/about/laws/ada-amendments.htm.

Afterschool Alliance. *21st Century Community Learning Centers Federal Afterschool Initiative* 2009. Available from http://www.afterschoolalliance.org/policy21stcclc.cfm.

Bagenholm, A., and C. Gillberg. 1991. Psychosocial effects on siblings with children with autism and mental retardation: A population-based study. *Journal of Mental Deficiency* 35:291-307.

Bagenstos, S.R. 2004. The future of disability law. *The Yale Law Review* 114 (1):1-83.

Barnett, RC, and KC Gareis. 2006. Parental after-school stress and psychological well-being. *Journal of Marriage and Family* 68 (1):101-108.

Barnett, W. S., D. J. Epstein, A. H. Friedman, R. A. Sansanelli, and J. T. Hustedt. 2009. *The state of preschool 2009: state preschool yearbook*: National Institute for Early Education Research.

Barnett, W.S. 1992. Benefits of compensatory preschool education. *The Journal of Human Resources* 27 (2):279-312.

Blau, D. 2001. *The child care problem: an economic analysis.* New York, NY: Russell Sage Foundation.

Blau, D, and E Tekin. 2007. The determinants and consequences of child care subsidies for single mothers in the USA. *Journal of Population Economics* 20 (4):719-741.

Blau, D. M., and P.K. Robins. 1998. Child care costs and family labor supply. *The Review of Economics and Statistics* 70 (3):297-316.

Blaxill, M. 2004. What's going on? The question of time trends in autism. *Public Health Reports* 119 (6):536-551.

Bouder, J. N., S. Spielman, and D. S. Mandell. 2009. Brief report: quantifying the impact of autism coverage on private insurance premiums. *Journal of Autism & Developmental Disorders* 39 (6):953-957.

Brandon, P. D. 2000. Child care utilization among working mothers raising children with disabilities. *Journal of Family and Economic Issues* 21:343-364.

Brandon, P. D., and S. L. Hofferth. 2003. Determinants of out-of-school childcare arrangements among children in single-mother and two-parent families. *Social Science Research* 32:129-147.

Browne Miller, A. 1990. *The day care dilemma: critical concerns for American families.* New York: Plenum Press.

Buck, KA, and RJ Ambrosino. 2004. Children with Severe Behavior Problems: A Survey of Texas Child Care Centers' Responses. *Early Childhood Education Journal* 31 (4):241-246.

Buckley, T. E. 2004. A mandate for anti-catholicism: the Blaine Amendment. *America* 181 (8):18-21.

References

Burchinal, M., K. Kainz, K. Cai, K. Tout, M. Zaslow, I. Martinez-Beck, and C. Rathgeb. 2009. *Early care and education quality and child outcomes*. Office of Planning, Research and Evaluation, Administration for Children and Families. Available from http://www.researchconnections.org/files/childcare/pdf/OPRERestoPolicyBrief1_FINAL.pdf.

Buysse, V., P. W. Wesley, D. Bryant, and D. Gardner. 1999. Quality of early childhood settings in inclusive and non-inclusive settings. *Children and Youth Services Review* 26:941-964.

Ceglowski, D., and C. Bacigalupa. 2002. Four perspectives on child care quality. *Early Childhood Research Quarterly* 30 (2):87-92.

Centers for Disease Control and Prevention (CDC). 2009. Prevalence of autism spectrum disorders - Autism and developmental disabilities monitoring network. *MMWR Surveillance Summary* 58 (10):1-20.

Chaudry, A., J. Henly, and M. Meyers. 2010. Conceptual frameworks for child care decision-making. Washington, DC: US Department of Health and Human Services. Office of Planning, research and Evaluation, Administration for Children and Families.

Chien, N.C., C. Howes, M. Burchinal, R.C. Pianta, S. Ritchie, D.M. Bryant, R.M. Clifford, D.M. Early, and O.A. Barbarin. 2010. Children's classroom engagement and school readiness gains in prekindergarten. *Child Development* 81 (5):1534-1549.

Child Care Bureau. 2011. *Child Care and Development Fund Fact Sheet*. Available from http://www.acf.hhs.gov/programs/occ/ccdf/factsheet.htm.

Clark, S.C. 2001. Work cultures and work/family balance. *Journal of Vocational Behavior* 58 (3):348-365.

Cleveland, G., M. Gunderson, and D. Hyatt. 1996. Child care costs and the employment decision of women: Canadian evidence. *Canadian Journal of Economics* 29 (1):132-151.

Connelly, R., and J. Kimmel. 2003. Marital status and full-time/part-time work status in child care choices. *Applied Economics* 35 (7):761-777.

Constantino, J. N., M. S. Yi Zhang, T. Fraizer, A. M. Abbacchi, and P. Law. 2010. Sibling recurrence and the genetic epidemiology of autism. *American Journal of Psychiatry* 167 (11):1349.

Cryer, D., and M. Burchinal. 1997. Parents as child care consumers. *Early Childhood Research Quarterly* 12:35-58.

Cryer, D., W. Tietze, and H. Wessels. 2002. Parents' perceptions of their children's child care: a cross-national comparison. *Early Childhood Research Quarterly* 17:259-277.

Currie, J, and D. Thomas. 1995. Does Head Start make a difference? *American Economic Review* 85 (3):341-64.

Cuskelly, M., L. Pulman, and A. Hayes. 1998. Parenting and employment decisions of parents with a preschool child with a disability. *Journal of Intellectual and Developmental Disability* 23: 319-333.

Danziger, S.K., E.O. Ananat, and K.G. Browning. 2006. Child-care subsidies and the transition from welfare to work. In *From welfare to child care: What happens to young children when single mothers exchange welfare for work?*, edited by N. Cabrera, R. Hutchens and H.E. Peters. Mahwah, NJ: Lawrence Erlbaum Associates Inc.

DeForrest, M E. 2003. An overview and evaluation of state Blaine Amendments: origins, scope and First Amendment concerns. *Harvard Journal of Law and Public Policy* 26 (2):551-626.

Dowding, K., P. John, T. Mergoupis, and M. van Vugt. 2000. Exit, voice and loyalty: Analytic and empirical developments. *European Journal of Empirical Research* 37 (4):469-495.

Dynarski, M., S. James-Burdumy, M. Moore, L. Rosenberg, J. Deke, and W. Mansfield. 2004. *When Schools Open Late: The National Evaluation of the 21st Century Community Learning Centers Programs: New Findings.* Washington, DC: US Government Printing Office.

Ellingsater, A.L. 2007. Old and New politics of time to care: three Norwegian reforms. *Journal of European Social Policy* 17:49-60.

Ellsworth Associates Inc. 1994. *Head Start research from 1985 to 1994: An annotated bibliography.* Washington, DC: US Department of Health and Human Services, Head Start Bureau.

Emlen, A. C. 2010. *Solving the childcare and flexibility puzzle: how working parents make the best feasible choices and what that means for public policy.* Boca Raton, FL: Universal Publishers.

Esenwein, G.A. *Child tax credit* 2010. Available from http://www.taxpolicycenter.org/taxtopics/encyclopedia/Child-Tax-Credit.cfm.

Esping-Anderson, G. 1999. *Social foundations of post-industrial economics.* Oxford, UK: Oxford University Press.

Etscheidt, S. 2003. An Analysis of Legal Hearings and Cases Related to Individualized Education Programs for Children with Autism. *Research and Practice for Persons with Severe Disabilities* 28 (2):51-69.

Fommbonne, E. 2003. The prevalence of autism. *JAMA* 289:87-89.

Fuller, B., S.D. Holloway, and X. Liang. 1996. Family selection of child care centers: the influence of household support, ethnicity and parental practices. *Child Development* 67 (6):3320-3337.

Furaker, B. 2009. Unsatisfactry working conditions and voice: An analysis involving employees in Sweden. *Journal of Workplace Rights* 14 (2):157-173.

GAO. 2010. *Child care and development fund: undercover tests show five state programs are vulnerable to fraud and abuse.* Vol. GAO-10-1062. Washington, DC: GAO.

Gilliam, W., and G. Shahar. 2006. Prekindergarten expulsion and suspension: rates and predictors in one state. *Infants and Young Children* 19 (3):228-245.

Gold, N. 1993. Depression and social adjustment in siblings of boys with autism. *Journal of Autism & Developmental Disorders* 23:147-163.

Goldrick-Rab, S. *The child-care crisis.* Chronicle of Higher Education 2010. Available from http://chronicle.com/blogs/brainstorm/the-child-care-crisis/21368.

Greenberg, P. 1990. *The devil has slippery shoes: a biased biography of the Child Development Group of Mississippi (CDGM): a story of maximum feasible poor parent participation.* Washington, DC: Youth Policy Institute.

Greenhaus, J.H., K.M. Collins, and J.D. Shaw. 2003. The relation between work-family balance and quality of life. *Journal of Vocational Behavior* 63 (3):510-531.

Gross, N., and S. Simmons. 2007. *The social and political views of American professors.* Cambridge: Harvard University Working paper.

References

Hacsi, T.A. 2002. *Children as Pawns: The Politics of Educational Reform*. Cambridge: Harvard University Press.

Hamilton, R.F., and L.L. Hargens. 1993. The politics of the professors: Self-identifications, 1969-1984. *Social Forces* 71 (3):603-627

Han, W., and J. Waldfogel. 2001. The effect of child care costs on the employment of single and married mothers. *Social Science Quarterly* 82 (3):552-568.

Han, W., and J. Waldvogel. 2003. Parental leave: the impact of recent legislation on parents' leave taking. *Demography* 40 (1):191-200.

Harmon, C. 2004. Was Head Start a community action program? Another look at an old debate. In *The Head Start Debates*, edited by E. Zigler and S.J. Styfco. Baltimore, MD: Paul H. Brookes Publishing Co.

Henderson, T.L., P.A. Monroe, J.C. Garand, and D.C. Burts. 1995. Explaining public opinion toward government spending on child care. *Family Relations* 44:37-45.

Henry, G.T., C.S. Gordon, and D.K. Rickman. 2006. Early education policy alternatives: comparing quality and outcomes of Head Start and State Prekindergarten. *Educational Evaluation and Policy Analysis* 28 (1):77-99.

Hill, E.J., A.J. Hawkins, M. Ferris, and M. Weitzman. 2004. Finding an extra day a week: The positive influence of perceived job flexibility on work and family life balance. *Family Relations* 50 (1):49-58.

Hill, E.J., V.K. Martinson, M. Ferris, and R.Z. Baker. 2004. Beyond the mommy track: The influence of new-concept part-time work for professional women on work and family. *Journal of Family and Economic Issues* 25 (1):121-136.

Hirschman, A. O. 1970. *Exit, voice and loyalty: responses to decline in firms, organizations and states.* Cambridge, MA: Harvard University Press.

Holland, C. D. 2010. Autism, insurance, and the idea: providing a comprehensive legal framework. *Cornell Law Review* 95 (6):1253-1282.

Hood, J. 1992. *Caveat Emptor: The Head Start Scam.* 187. Available from http://www.cato.org/pubs/pas/pa187.pdf.

Howard, C. 2003. Is the American welfare state unusually small? *Political science and politics* 36 (3):411-416.

Hudelson, R. 1998. *Modern political philosophy.* Armonk, NY: M.E.Sharpe, Inc.

Interagency Autism Coordinating Committee. 2009. 2009 Summary of Advances in Autism Spectrum Disorder Research. Washington, DC

Interagency Autism Coordinating Committee. *2010 Strategic plan for autism spectrum disorder research* 2010 [cited December 2010. Available from http://iacc.hhs.gov/strategic-plan/2010/index.shtml.

IRS. *Top ten facts about the child and dependent care credit* 2010. Available from http://www.irs.gov/newsroom/article/0,,id=106189,00.html.

———. *Topic 602 - Child and Dependent Care Credit* 2010. Available from http://www.irs.gov/taxtopics/tc602.html.

Jacoby, W.G. 2000. Issue framing and public opinion on government spending. *American Journal of Political Science* 44 (4):750-767.

Johansen, A. S., and A. Leibowitz. 1996. The importance of child-care characteristics to choice of care. *Journal of Marriage and Family* 58:759-773.

Kagan, R. A., and L. Axelrad. 1997. Adversarial legalism: an international perspective. In *Comparative disadvantages? Social regulations and the new economy*, edited by P. S. Nivola. Washington, DC: Brookings Institution.

Kanner, L. 1943. Autistic disturbances of affective contact. *Nervous Child* 2:217-250.

Kendler, K. S. 2010. Advances in our understanding of genetic risk factors for autism spectrum disorders. *American Journal of Psychiatry* 167:1291-1293.

Kesinger Rose, K., and J. Elicker. 2008. Parental decision making about child care. *Journal of Family Issues* 29:1161-1184.

Kimmel, J. 1995. The effectiveness of child care subsidies in encouraging the welfare to work transitions of low-income single mothers. *American Economic Review* 85 (2):271-275.

King, M., and P. Bearman. 2009. Diagnostic change and the increased prevalence of autism. *International Journal of Epidemiology* 38:1224-1234.

Klein, A. G. 1992. *The debate over child care: a sociohistorical analysis*. Albany, NY: State University of New York Press.

Klein, D. B., and C. Stern. 2008. Liberal versus conservative stinks. *Society* 45:488-495.

Klein, D.B., and C. Stern. 2005. Political diversity in six disciplines. *Academic questions* 18 (1):40-52.

Klein, D.B., and C. Stern. 2005. Professors and their politics: the policy views of social scientists. *Critical Review: an Interdisciplinary Journal of Politics and Society* 17 (3&4):257-303.

Kuhn, T. S. 1962. *The structure of scientific revolutions.* Chicago, IL: University of Chicago Press.

Kuntz, K.R. 1998. A lost legacy: Head Start's origins in community action. In *Critical perspectives on Project Head Start: Revisioning the hope and challenge*, edited by J. Ellsworth and L. J. Ames. Albany, NY: State University of New York.

Kutz, G. D. *Head Start: Undercover testing finds fraud and abuse at selected Head Start centers, testimony before the Committee on Education and Labor, US House of Representatives* 2010. Available from www.gao.gov/new.items/d10733t.pdf.

Langston, J. 2002. Breaking out is hard to do: Exit, voice and loyalty in Mexico's one-party hegemonic regime. *Latin American Politics and Society* 44 (3):61-88.

Larner, M., and D. Phillips. 1994. Defining and valuing quality as a parent. In *Valuing quality in early child care services: New approaches to defining quality*, edited by P. Moss and A. Pence. London: Paul Chapman Press.

Lawrence, S., and J. Lee Kreader. 2005. *Predictors of child care subsidy use.* New York: Child Care and Early Education Research Connections.

Lee, V., J. Brooks-Gunn, E. Schnur, and F.R. Liaw. 1990. Are Head Start effects sustained? A longitudinal follow-up comparison of disadvantaged children attending Head Start, no preschool and other preschool programs. *Child Development* 61:495-507.

Lee, V., and S. Loeb. 1995. Where do Head Start attendees end up? One reason why preschool effects fade out. *Educational Evaluation and Policy Analysis* 17 (1):62-82.

Lewis, J. 2009. Balancing time to work and time to care: policy issues and the implications for mothers, fathers and children. *Child and Family Law Quarterly* 21 (4):443-461.

Liptak, G. S., T. Stuart, and P. Auinger. 2006. Health care utilization and expenditures for children with autism: data from US national samples. *Journal of Autism & Developmental Disorders* 36 (7):871-879.

Macks, R.J., and R.E. Reeve. 2007. The adjustment of non-disabled siblings of children with autism. *Journal of Autism & Developmental Disorders* 37:1060-1067.

Mates, T.E. 1990. Siblings of autistic children: Their adjustment and performance at home and in school. *Journal of Autism & Developmental Disorders* 20 (4):545-553.

Mazumdar, S., M. King, K. Liu, N. Zerubavel, and P. Bearman. 2009. The spatial structure of autism in California, 1993-2001. *Health & Place* 16 (3):539-546.

Mazumder, B. 2005. Fortunate sons: new estimates of intergenerational mobility in the United States using social security earnings data. *The Review of Economics and Statistics* 87 (2):235-255.

McClure, R. *Is there a crisis with child care?* 2011. Available from http://childcare.about.com/od/costofchildcare/a/crisis.htm.

McKenna, C. 2010. Child care subsidies in the United States: Government Funding to Families (2010). In *Work and family encyclopedia*, edited by S. Sweet and J. Casey. Chestnut Hill, MA: Sloan Work and Family Research Network.

Meyers, M. K., and L. P. Jordan. 2006. Choice and accomodation in parental child care decisions. *Community Development* 37 (2):53-70.

Meyers, M.K., and A. Durfee. 2006. Who pays? The visible and invisible costs of child care. *Politics and Society* 34:109-128.

Michalopoulos, C., and P.K. Robins. 2002. Employment and childcare choices of single parent families in Canada and the United States. *Journal of Population Economics* 15:465-493.

MomsRising. *The crisis of American Families and the Bias Against Mothers* 2011. Available from http://www.momsrising.org/crisis-bias.

Montes, G. 1996. Public funding and institutional reorganization: Evidence from the early kindergarten movement. *Nonprofit management and leadership* 7 (4):405-420.

Montes, G., and J. S. Halterman. 2008. Association of childhood autism spectrum disorders and loss of family income. *Pediatrics* 121 (4):e821-6.

Montes, G., and J. S. Halterman. 2008. Child care problems and employment among families with preschool-aged children with autism in the United States. *Pediatrics* 122 (1):e202-8.

Montes, G., and J.S. Halterman. 2011. The impact of child care problems on employment: findings from a national survey of US parents. *Academic Pediatrics* 11 (1):80-87.

Murphy, A. P., and L. Lacy. *More parents face a child care crisis: Families turn to relatives to pick up the slack.* 2009. Available from http://abcnews.go.com/GMA/Parenting/parents-face-child-care-crisis/story?id=6711684.

National Council on Disabilities. *Back to School on Civil Rights* 2000. Available from http://www.ncd.gov/newsroom/publications/2000/pdf/backtoschool.pdf.

Naumann, I.K. 2005. Child care and feminism in West Germany and Sweden in the 1960s and 1970s. *Journal of European Social Policy* 15:47-63.

Ng, G.T. 2006. Child care in the United States: Who shapes state policies for children? *Social Work Research* 30 (2):71-81.

NICHD Early Child Care Research Network. 1997. Child care in the first year of life. *Merrill Palmer Quarterly* 43 (3):340-360.

Office of Child Care. 2008. *Child care and development fund (CCDF) report to Congress for FY 2006 and FY 2007.* Available from http://www.acf.hhs.gov/programs/occ/ccdf/rtc/rtc2006/rtc_2006_2007.pdf.

Office of Head Start - Administration for Children and Families. *Head Start Program Fact Sheet* 2010. Available from www.acf.hhs.gov/programs/ohs/about/fy2010.html.

Okamoto, D. G., and R. Wilkes. 2008. The opportunities and costs of voice and exit: modeling ethnic group rebellion and emigration. *Journal of Ethnic and Migration Studies* 34 (3):347-369.

Opinion Research Corporation International. 1999. *Fight crime: invest in kids back to to school poll.* Washington, DC: Opinion Research International.

Parish, S. L., and J. M. Cloud. 2005. Child care for low-income school-age children: disability and family structure effects in a national sample. *Children and Youth Services Review* 28:927-940.

Parish, S. L., J. M. Cloud, J. Huh, and A. S. Henning. 2005. Child care, disability, and family structure: Use and quality in a population-based sample of low-income preschool children. *Children and Youth Services Review* 27:905-919.

Pierson, P. 2000. Increasing returns, path dependence and the study of politics. *The American Political Science Review* 94 (2):251-267.

Powell, L.M. 2002. Joint labor supply and childcare choice decisions of married mothers. *Journal of Human Resources* 37 (1):106-128.

Public Agenda. 2000. *Necessary compromises: How parents, employers, and children's advocates view child care today.* New York: Public Agenda.

Rell, M.J. 2007. *Testimony of Governor M. Jodi Rell supporting S.B. 1114: An Act Implementing the Governor's Budget Recommendations Regarding Education 2007.* Available from http://www.ct.gov/governorrell/cwp/view.asp?A=1809&Q=332800.

Robison, J. 2002. *Should mothers work?* Princeton, NJ: The Gallup Corporation.

Rose, K. K., and J. Elicker. 2008. Parental decision making about child care. *Journal of Family Issues* 29 (9):1161-1184.

Rosenberg, R. 1992. *Divided lives: American women in the twentieth century.* New York: Hill and Wang.

Rosenzweig, J. M., E. M. Brennan, K. Huffstutter, and J. R. Bradley. 2008. Child care and employed parents of children with emotional or behavioral disorders. *Journal of Emotional and Behavioral Disorders* 16 (2):78-89.

Rosenzweig, J. M., E. M. Brennan, and A. M. Ogilivie. 2002. Work-family fit: voices of parents of children with emotional and behavioral disorders. *Social Work* 47 (4):415-424.

Ross, E. D. 1976. *Kindergarten crusade: the establishment of preschool education in the United States.* Athens, OH: Ohio University Press.

Ryan, R. M., A. Johnson, E. Rigby, and J Brooks-Gunn. 2011. The impact of child care subsidy use on child care quality. *Early Childhood Research Quarterly* 26 (3):320-331.

Saunders, J. B. 2010. Overwhelmed by autism: a dramatic increase in diagnoses has lawmakers debating the state's role. *State Legis* 36 (9):36-39.

Schaefer, S.A., J. Lee Kreader, and A.M. Collins. 2005. *Predictors of child care subsidy use.* New York: Child care and early education research connections.

Seo, S. 2003. Early child care choices: A theoretical model and research implications. *Early child development and care* 173 (6): 637-650.

Shearn, J., and S. Todd. 2000. Maternal employment and family responsibilities. *Journal of Applied Research in Intellectual Disabilities* 13:109-131.

Shipley, T. E. 2001. Child care centers and children with special needs: Rights under the Americans with Disabilities Act and Section 504 of the Rehabilitation Act. *Journal of Law and Education* 31 (3):327-349.

Shlay, A. B., M. Weinraub, M. Harmon, and H. Tran. 2002. *Barriers to subsidies: Reasons why low-income families do not use child care subsidies*. Philadelphia: Temple University Center for Public Policy.

Shlay, A. B., M. Weinraub, M. Harmon, and H. Tran. 2004. Barriers to subsidies: Why low-income families do not use child care subsidies. *Social Science Research* 33 (1):134-157.

Smith, K. 2000. Who's minding the kids? Child care arrangements, Fall 1995. Current Population Reports, P70-90. Washington, DC: US Census Bureau.

Solon, G. 2002. Cross-country differences in intergerational earnings mobility. *Journal of Economic Perspectives* 16 (3):59-66.

Sylvester, K. 2001. Caring for our youngest: Public attitudes in the United States. *The Future of Children* 11 (1):52-61.

Tausig, M., and R. Fenwick. 2001. Unbinding time: Alternative work schedules and work-life balance. *Journal of Family and Economic Issues* 22 (2):101-119.

US Department of Education. 2010. *US Department of Education determination letters on state implementation of IDEA* 2008. Available from http://www2.ed.gov/print/policy/speced/guid/idea/monitor/factsheet.html.

U.S. General Accounting Office. 2003. *Child care: recent policy changes affecting availability of assistance for low-income families*. Vol. GAO-03-588. Washington, DC: US General Accounting Office.

United States Administration for Children and Families. 2007. Patterns of child care use among low income families: final report. Washington, DC: US Administration for Children and Families.

United States Government Accountability Office. 2009. Seclusions and restraints: selected cases of death and abuse at public and private schools and treatment centers. Washington, DC.

US Department of Education. *21st Century Community Learning Centers: Non Statutory Guidance* 2003. Available from http://sde.state.ok.us/Finance/21stCent/pdf/21CentGuide.pdf.

US Department of Health and Human Services. 2010. Administration of Children and Families. *Head Start impact study: final report* 2010. Available from www.acf.hhs.gov/programs/opre/hs/impact_study/reports/impact_study/hs_impact_study_final.pdf.

US Department of Justice. 2010. *Commonly asked questions about child care centers and the American with Disabilities Act* 2010]. Available from http://www.ada.gov/childq%26a.htm.

Vincent, C., and S. J. Ball. 2006. *Childcare, Choice and Class Practices: Middle Class Parents and Their Children.* London, UK: Routledge.

Waldvogel, J. 1999. The impact of the Family and Medical Leave Act. *Journal of Policy Analysis and Management* 18 (2):281-302.

Ward, H., L. Morris, J. Atkins, A. Herrick, and P. Morris. 2006. Child care and children with special needs: challenges for low income families. Portland, ME: Edmund S. Muskie School of Public Service, University of Southern Maine.

White, L.A. 2002. Ideas and the welfare state: Explaining child care policy development in Canada and the United States. *Comparative Political Studies* 35:713-743.

White, L.A. 2009. Explaining differences in child care policy development in France and the USA: Norms, frames and programmatic ideas. *International Political Science Review* 30:385-405.

Wilson, D. 2009. Exit, voice and quality in the English education sector. *Social policy & Administration* 43 (6):571-584.

Zigler, E. 1990. Shaping child care policies and programs in America. *American Journal of Community Psychology* 18 (2):183-216.

Zigler, E., and M. E. Lang. 1991. *Child care choices: Balancing the needs of children, families and society.* New York: The Free Press.

Zigler, E., K. Marsland, and H. Lord. 2009. *The tragedy of child care in America.* New Haven, CT: Yale University Press.

Zigler, E., and S. Muenchow. 1994. *Head Start: The inside story of America's most succesful educational experiment*: Basic Books.

Zigler, E., and S. J. Styfco. 2004. The wisdom of a federal effort on behalf of impoverished children and their families. In *The Head Start Debates*, edited by E. Zigler and S. J. Styfco. Baltimore, MD: Paul H. Brookes Publishing Company.

Zigler, E., and J. Valentine. 1979. *Project Head Start: A legacy of the War on Poverty.* New York: The Free Press.

Zinzeleta, E., and N. K. Little. 1997. How do parents really choose early childhood programs? *Young children* 52 (7):8-11.

Zipp, J.F., and R. Fenwick. 2006. Is the academy a liberal hegemony? The political orientations and educational values of professors. *Public opinion quarterly* 70 (3):304-326.

Zraik, T. 2011. *Jordan Burriola vs. Greater Toledo YMCA: Why this case is important.* 2011. Available from www.wrightslaw.com.

www.ingramcontent.com/pod-product-compliance
Lightning Source LLC
Chambersburg PA
CBHW041616220426
43671CB00001B/7